# Dick and I

# Dick and I

## Our First Twenty-seven Years
## as Twin Brothers and Best Friends

**Jack Horrigan**

*To Cathy, Rich, Ann Louise, Peter,*
*David, Jimmy, Kate, Matt and Chris*
*in memory of your dad.*

There is nothing that can replace the absence of someone dear to us, and one should not even attempt to do so. One must simply hold out and endure it. At first that sounds very hard, but at the same time it is also a great comfort. For to the extent the emptiness truly remains unfilled one remains connected to the other person through it. It is wrong to say that God fills the emptiness. God in no way fills it but much more leaves it precisely unfilled and thus helps us preserve —even in pain—the authentic relationship. Furthermore, the more beautiful and full the remembrances, the more difficult the separation. But gratitude transforms the torment of memory into silent joy. One bears what was lovely in the past not as a thorn but as a precious gift deep within, a hidden treasure of which one can always be certain.

— *Dietrich Bonhoeffer*

# Contents

# Acknowledgments

First and foremost I'd like to thank my children—Mary Jo, Suzanne, Betsy, John, Karen and Patrick—for their support and encouragement in the preparation of this book.

Particular thanks to Karen and Betsy for keeping me focused, following every detail, and managing the entire process. I could not have done it without them.

Additional thanks to my granddaughter Erin for her editorial assistance.

And finally, there are several others I would like to thank: Dick's wife, Dolores, for sharing countless photos; my sisters—Mary O'Connell, Theresa Montgomery, Peggy Connolly, Maddie Horrigan, and Sue Ozar—for the photos they provided; Joan Cunningham, Barbara Fahy and Frank Mulligan for their helpful edits; and Tom Fenton, publisher, for bringing Dick's and my story to life.

# Prologue

THIS BOOK CHRONICLES THE VERY CLOSE RELATIONSHIP Dick and I shared as twin brothers. We were together virtually every day during the first twenty-seven years of our lives, including attending school from first grade through high school and college. After college graduation I began working in Philadelphia in the consumer finance business while Dick, living at home in Reading, Pennsylvania, worked in the automobile finance business. I returned home every weekend for a year and a half until we were drafted during the Korean War. We served together in the U.S. Army, living in shared quarters for the entire two years of military service. Upon discharge we remained together, living back home as we resumed our careers, until our respective weddings.

This was a period of sharing, personal growth, friendship, challenges, mutual support and new experiences. You might imagine that these shared experiences and challenges could have contributed to a certain mutual dependency; rather, the certainty that we were there for each other contributed to our sense of self-confidence. We regarded these twenty-seven years together as a privilege and knew from an early age how fortunate we were to have each other as brothers and best friends.

As the eldest of eight children, our lives together with Mary, Theresa, Peggy, Maddie, Sue, Mike and our parents (the "Horrigan Family") spanned a very interesting and tempestuous time in our country's history. We learned the value of personal honor, respect for others, hard work, patience and love by witnessing how our parents lived their lives. Mom and Pop instilled important character attributes in their children early on. Dick and I were blessed to have their mutual reaffirmation throughout our lives together.

I begin this narrative by introducing Mom and Pop—where they were born and how they met—followed by details of our birth and very early life, as gleaned from information shared by our parents and others of their generation. Thereafter, the memories are mine alone, as I never had the opportunity to share with Dick the possibility of recording our mutual life experiences. I understand the reality of selective recall, but have done my best to be accurate and objective.

# 1

# We Are Family

OUR MOTHER, MADELINE, was born in Reading and was the seventh of John A. and Theresa (Gruber) Rauen's nine children. Our father, John, was the third of John F. and Hanna (Desmond) Horrigan's five children and was born in Baltimore, Maryland. They met during the summer of 1924 when Pop came to Reading with his Baltimore buddy Ray Philbin for a weekend of AAA International League baseball games between the Baltimore Orioles and the Reading Keys. Family lore has it that Pop and Ray met Mom's sister (Aunt Peg) on Sunday morning at St. Peter Church in Reading, and she invited them to have breakfast at the Rauen family home a block away. It was there that Mom and Pop first met and began a long-distance courtship that culminated in their marriage several years later.

On October 15, 1928, Dick I and were born several months prematurely at St. Joseph Hospital in Reading. I am not sure if twins were expected—let alone identical twins. Certainly our gender was unknown until birth since advanced imaging and neonatal care innovations were still far in the future. I was born first and named John Francis after Pop. Dick was born ten minutes after me and was named Richard Walter after Pop's younger brother Walter Richard.

We each weighed no more than a few pounds and it was said that we could fit together in a cigar box. As a result of the premature birth, Dick's head and chin were underdeveloped, with an opening on top of his head the width of two fingers. I was frail as well although somewhat more developed than Dick. Mom always said that if it had not been for the nurturing love and care of Mary Boland, a nurse at the hospital, we would not have survived. Mom's obstetrician, Dr. Leon Darrah, had not expected us to live, and whenever he saw Dick and me thereafter, he marveled at our survival.

We remained in the hospital for weeks and were fed like birds with a dropper. This feeding method continued hourly after we returned home. Mom and Pop were understandably overwhelmed by the enormity of their new responsibilities. Many family members—including Mom's sisters Hilda, Claire and Peg—helped care for us during sleepless days and nights. Their love, dedication, patience and determination ultimately prevailed.

Like many young new parents, Mom and Pop moved several times to strike the appropriate balance between housing affordability and room for their growing family. Our first home after leaving the hospital was an apartment at 2404 Filbert Street in Mt. Penn. We moved a bit later to a house in the 400 block of Broad Street in Shillington. While living there, our sister Mary was born, on February 22, 1930. Mary was sixteen months younger than Dick and me, but since we were born prematurely and were slow to develop, Mom was literally caring for three babies at one time. She had her hands full preparing and managing three sets of formula, changing and washing endless cloth diapers and the like. Mom was fortunate, however, to have live-in help; the 1930 U.S. Census report indicates that fifteen-year-old Helen Andrulus also lived with us during this time. Our country was in the midst of the "Great Depression" and it was not uncommon for families to hire a live-in helper for bed, board and a modest salary.

Our family then moved to a town house in the 2500 block of Grant Street in Mt. Penn. It was while living there that our sister Theresa was born, on October 17, 1932.

## 2

# 3400 Perkiomen Avenue

IN 1933 OUR FAMILY OF SIX MOVED TO A LARGER HOME in Reiffton, at 3400 Perkiomen Avenue. This was the first home in which I can recall living: a three-story frame house with a basement garage and rather large backyard. As five-year-olds, Dick and I were home all day since there was no preschool or kindergarten at the time. Incredibly, Mom was able to manage the curiosity and activities of three little ones while also caring for a new baby.

Our neighborhood was friendly and, as luck would have it, we had built-in playmates with our immediate neighbors, the Wertz family. Allen and Marie Wertz had four children: Bud, Karl, Joan and Jean. Jean was the same age as Dick and me and was our sister Mary's friend, so the four of us spent a lot of time together playing hide-and-seek, tag and other outdoor games. Between our homes was a large lot with a fenced-in area for their dog, Ritz, a beautiful and friendly Dalmatian.

Mr. Wertz was an excellent candy maker; he worked for Zipf's Candies, a very successful business in Reading that

3400 Perkiomen Avenue

operated a number of retail stores in the area. Mr. Wertz also made homemade ice cream and often shared his recipes with our family. Our favorite flavors were peach and chocolate.

At the end of our backyard was an alley leading up a hill to Reed's grocery store on West 33rd Street. In the 1930s there were few large grocery chains such as those familiar to us today. Groceries and dry goods were purchased from small, family-run stores such as Reed's. For Dick and me, a trip to Reed's was truly something to be savored.

As we walked into the store it would be common to greet neighbors completing their purchases—perhaps even sharing a bit of local news to be passed back to Mom. Reed's was an old-fashioned general store with large wooden tubs of coffee and other bulk items and shelves stacked high with canned food and dry goods. Of particular distinction, Reed's served as the Reiffton Post Office. Dick and I often purchased various foods for Mom and picked up the mail as well.

Of course Dick and I had dual intentions when dispatched to Reed's: fill Mom's grocery order but more importantly purchase a sampling of their penny candy. The candy was located in a glass-enclosed cabinet adjacent to the cash register to ensure appropriate supervision by the cashier. Dick and I worked well together, scanning the candy selection and making our purchase with minimal interruption to other customers.

Family-owned grocery stores and the experiences shared within are vestiges of American culture no longer with us. Their presence in America during the Great Depression of the 1930s represented a significant lifeline for many families who required assistance extended by the kindness of the Reeds and other local grocery store owners. The location itself served vital social interests for shared news in the community and the various fortunes and misfortunes of families making their way in the midst of the most challenging time our country had ever experienced.

In 1935, the Wertz family sold their home and all their possessions and drove to Los Angeles to start a new life. Mr. Wertz established a candy factory there and opened a store on Wilshire Boulevard. It was not uncommon in those days for families to make similar moves, since economic opportunity was still scarce in the waning days of the Depression. It was a sad day for the Horrigan kids when our best friends left town.

The Wertz's home was purchased by Agnes and Jess James, who in addition to being neighbors became good family friends. Mrs. James was Mom's bridge-playing friend. Mr. James was a very personable, funny man who always had stories to share with Dick and me. He claimed to be a close friend of Knute Rockne, the famous Notre Dame football coach at the time. He convinced us that he spoke with Rockne every Friday during the season to get the lowdown on the next day's game. As seven-year-old boys, Dick and I believed everything he said to be true.

# 3

## Uncle Walter

POP'S YOUNGER BROTHER, WALTER, LIVED WITH US for approximately seven years until Dick and I were eleven years old. Uncle Walter was always fun to be with—a storyteller, magician, card player, comedian, musician and occasional babysitter. Uncle Walter worked for Pop's finance company, J. F. Horrigan Co., as a collector of delinquent automobile and truck finance accounts. Automobiles had been in mass production for about fifteen years by this time and their utility continued to astound. Professionals, doctors, laborers—people of all walks of life—wanted and needed an automobile, if they could afford it.

Uncle Walter would often leave home for several days at a time to visit accounts in the "coal regions," an area in upstate Pennsylvania aptly named because of its vast deposits of anthracite coal. With the Depression in full swing, a number of the accounts would become delinquent and require personal contact. Dick and I always looked forward to Uncle Walter's return, since he often had new stories to share with us. He was a natural storyteller and these trips provided him the opportunity to replenish his repertoire of stories—likely a hybrid of truthful witness and a bit of exaggeration.

Uncle Walter was also an occasional Friday night bingo player. Upon returning home, he would place his winnings—usually canned goods or other practical items—in the living room for us to see. The next morning we couldn't wait to discover what he had won.

Another fond memory of Uncle Walter was his key role in many Fourth of July celebrations, always a special day for our family. All of us—aunts, uncles, cousins and our maternal grandmother, MomMom—would gather for a backyard picnic each year. The picnic fare generally included plenty of hot dogs and hamburgers, as well as kegs of beer for the adults and soda for the kids. At sunset, the men, led by Uncle Walter, set off a huge fireworks display on the lot next to our home.

Backyard picnics were a rather common experience at the time. Depression-era life entailed a significant element of self-reliance. When families were confronted with the choice of spending limited funds on entertainment, they generally opted to make their own fun—rather simple days.

Uncle Walter and a buddy of his from Baltimore, George Winterling, joined the merchant marines, as many adventuresome, young men did in the 1920s. George was nicknamed "Doughy" since his dad was a baker. They were in Kobe, Japan, when Dick and I were born in 1928. Uncle Walter purchased two pairs of children's Oriental slippers for us. They were made of blue felt and had many sequins. Mom truly cherished the slippers.

Over the years we heard many stories about Doughy and his various escapades. In the 1950s, he opened a chain of three consumer loan offices in Lancaster County, Pennsylvania, under the name Amity Finance. As adults Dick and I became personal friends of Doughy given our common business interests. In 1971, newly elected Governor Milton Shapp appointed Doughy as Pennsylvania State Secretary of

Economic Development. After assuming his role in Governor Shapp's cabinet, Doughy called me one day and said, "Now that I'm a government official, the Statue of Justice here in Harrisburg has been blindfolded." Such was Doughy's great sense of humor!

# 4

## Grade School Years

IN THE FALL OF 1934, just shy of our sixth birthday, Dick and I
attended first grade at Reiffton Grade School. We were de-
lighted to finally be attending school! Dick and I loved our
teacher, Mrs. Boyer. We also loved to read. There were three
first-grade reading classes: Cardinals, Blue Jays and Chick-
adees. As good readers we were placed in the Cardinals.
Many years later, Dick and I were having lunch at the
Shillington Farmer's Market when an elderly lady asked if
we were the Horrigan boys. We recognized her as Mrs.
Boyer. It was quite a thrill to see her again, as she was one of
our favorite teachers.

Dick and I remained at Reiffton Grade School through
the sixth grade. I have vivid memories of our making many
new friends during our time there. We enjoyed all our teachers and classes and, as typical youngsters, eagerly
anticipated recess each day. I also recall that at the beginning of each school day our teacher led the entire class in a
prayer, the singing of a spiritual song and a patriotic song.
Can you imagine that in a public school today?

Dick and I never sensed that we were competing with each other. Mom and Pop encouraged us to do the best work we were capable of; they never made demands and they never drew comparisons. As it turned out, our marks were always good and quite similar. The only class with which we had difficulty was handwriting—the Palmer method was never our strength.

From our classroom we saw dozens of men from the Works Progress Administration (WPA) leveling the grounds behind the school with hand shovels to create a playing field. The WPA was a program established by the federal government in the early 1930s to provide employment. The leveled area later became the neighborhood athletic field, where we enjoyed many pick-up games until we left for college in 1946.

To prepare for our First Communion in the spring of 1935, Dick and I regularly attended Sunday school after the 9:00 A.M. Mass at St. Catharine [*sic*] of Siena Church in Mt. Penn. Since St. Catharine's did not have a grade school until 1938, the Immaculate Heart of Mary nuns from St. Joseph Parish in Reading would come to St. Catharine's to teach Sunday school and prepare us for First Communion. Coincidentally, our Sunday school teacher for the first several years was Sister John Elizabeth, who I discovered many years later also taught my wife, Peg, at St. Joseph Grade School. It's a small world—or at least a small town!

Our family remained members of St. Catharine's parish until Mom and Pop sold the family home in Reiffton in the mid-1970s and moved to the Wynnewood Apartments in Wyomissing, Pennsylvania.

# 5

# 3601 Perkiomen Avenue

WE MOVED TO 3601 PERKIOMEN AVENUE IN 1936. It was a much larger house on the corner of East 36th Street, across the highway from the Reiffton Grade School. Mom and Pop had purchased it from the Home Owners Loan Association, a federal agency that acquired and resold residential real estate foreclosed upon during the Depression. Walter Mountz, a local coal dealer, had built the home during the boom years in the mid-1920s. Sadly for him and his family, they were among the many who had fallen victim to the ravages of the Depression.

From the enclosed back porch of the house, you could access the kitchen, the laundry room and a full bathroom with an old-fashioned tub. The bathroom also connected with the kitchen. Apparently the configuration was designed to permit Mr. Mountz to enter the bathroom and bathe after his day's work, before entering the kitchen. Pop always referred to him as "Shorty" Mountz since the toilet in their bathroom was so low.

3601 Perkiomen Avenue

There was a full-tiled porch covering the entire front of the house paralleling Perkiomen Avenue. Red awnings were placed over the porch during the summertime. Behind the house was a detached two-car garage and rather large backyard.

Dick and I frequently climbed "the rocks" across the street from our home. The rocks were deposited there during the glacial age and created a perfect place for us to climb and play games such as hide-and-seek or Cowboys and Indians with neighborhood friends. We spent hours playing there and knew every crevice and hidden path, knew which rocks were loose and dangerous to step upon, where the snakes were, how to avoid poison ivy and in general how to play safely. This unusual rock formation is there to this day, and no doubt continues to be a special place for children to play.

There was also a large field adjacent to our house. In those days it was legal to burn leaves. On several occasions, while burning the raked leaves from our backyard, Dick and

I inadvertently started field fires and Reiffton firefighters had to be summoned. Finally, Pop put a stop to our burning leaves when the fire company refused to continue extinguishing the fires.

On September 5, 1936, when Dick and I were almost eight years old, our sister Peggy was born. Her birth coincided with Mom's brother Joe's wedding in Philadelphia. Pop was scheduled to be in Uncle Joe's wedding party, but returned home prior to the wedding to be with Mom. Ray Philbin, Pop's good friend from Baltimore, stood in for him at the wedding.

In the winter of 1938, our house was quarantined because one of our sisters had the mumps, a very communicable disease. A placard was placed at the front door and none of us could leave the house until he or she had contracted and recovered from the disease. One by one each of us contracted mumps—Dick and I were the last and did so simultaneously. As a result, we remained home from school and indoors for several months. We tried everything we could think of to keep active and stave off boredom. We would crawl under, in and around the wicker furniture that had been moved from the front porch to the basement for the winter months. We also read a lot, listened to the radio, played many card and board games and were provided homework from school on a daily basis. Dick and I were anxious to return to school, having been absent for more than a quarter of fourth grade. As bored as we were it must have been very difficult for Mom with everyone home sick from school for such a long time.

Our family continued to grow when Maddie was born on September 19, 1938, and Sue was born on April 4, 1941. Dick, Mary, Theresa and I were then referred to as the "older" children, while Peggy, Maddie and Sue were the "younger" children. The addition of two more sisters clearly added to the activity level within our home.

# 6

# World War II

ON THE AFTERNOON OF SUNDAY, DECEMBER 7, 1941, Dick and I were in the basement assembling the train yard with Pop while listening to the Philadelphia Eagles vs. Washington Redskins NFL football game when the broadcast was interrupted with the announcement that Pearl Harbor had been bombed by Japan. Pop said, "Boys, we are at war!" We were thirteen years old and in eighth grade at the time. Pop then talked with us about the implications of the bombing and what might be forthcoming. It was a very scary time indeed.

The next morning the school principal addressed an assembly of all the students. He compared World War II to a football game where we, the United States, had scored a touchdown (i.e., having won six previous wars) and were now preparing to kick the extra point by winning this new war. It was a very unusual analogy, but one, I suppose, the principal thought appropriate for children our age.

Air raid drills and blackouts became common activities, even though the United States had never experienced any air raids. Pop became a volunteer Air Raid Warden and was trained to identify enemy aircraft in flight. On late evening air raid drills, he would meet other volunteers at the Reiffton Fire Company and walk the neighborhood to ensure that lights were off or sufficiently dimmed during the blackout.

At home, we turned off all lights in the exterior rooms, and Mom, Dick, the five girls and I retreated to the second-floor hallway. All doors from the bedrooms and bathroom were closed, creating a space where light from a lamp was invisible to the outside. The only piece of furniture in the hall was a telephone stand and phone. While there, Mom led us in reciting the rosary as we waited for the air raid drill to end. It was difficult at times for Mom to maintain order as the seven of us became bored and impatient, with Dick and I expressing most of the impatience.

As the country was mobilizing for war, Americans at home were asked to do without most of the luxuries and many of the necessities that had begun to be in short supply. As a result, the federal government introduced a rationing system. It was the only way to ensure that everyone got his or her fair share. As an example, you couldn't simply walk into a shop and buy as much sugar, butter or meat as desired, nor could you fill up your car with gasoline whenever you ran low. Mom had an incredible ability to manage the food-rationing system for a family of nine. For Pop it was a concerted effort to juggle his basic and supplemental gasoline-rationing cards required to meet his business and family needs. (See Appendix, pp. 99–101.)

To supplement their food supply, many families had victory gardens to grow their own fresh vegetables. Our victory garden was in a corner of the field adjacent to our backyard. We grew corn, potatoes, beans, tomatoes, carrots and other vegetables. Dick and I were caretakers of the garden with help from the rest of the family.

# 7

# Life Goes On


DURING THE WAR IT WAS PATRIOTIC TO SAVE ITEMS such as rubber bands, cardboard and the tin foil from chewing gum and candy wrappers. The items would ultimately be collected at curbside and recycled for use during the war. We also saved all of our coins to purchase war stamps at the Reiffton Post Office—by then relocated from Reed's grocery store to the side porch of a private home on the corner of West 34th and James Streets. When sufficient stamps were accumulated we redeemed them for a war bond.

Our family lived frugally, but as children we were never aware of it. There was no television to show us what others had and conversely what we did not have. We did realize, however, that many families were not as fortunate, and Mom and Pop encouraged us to help others as much as possible. Frequently people would knock on the front door asking for food, and Mom would send them around to the back porch and give them something to eat. They often asked if they could do something around the house to return the favor. It was a time when people genuinely reached out to one another for help and did not necessarily expect the government to take care of all their needs.

One summer afternoon in the late 1930s, an organized march of about fifty people passed by our home. Bernarr Macfadden, a health and fitness advocate and owner of many publications, including the popular *Liberty* magazine, led a march that began in New York City en route to Washington, D.C. The march had received considerable publicity, most likely because of Macfadden's belief in exercise, good nutrition and body building. He was also a strong supporter of President Franklin D. Roosevelt and sought to be named to his cabinet. Knowing when the marchers would pass by our house, Mom encouraged us to watch from the sidewalk. Although in retrospect it may have been a publicity stunt to promote Macfadden's publications and fuel his political ambitions, it was quite fascinating to see the marchers as they passed by.

Economic times were certainly difficult, and as children, Dick and I received little or no allowance. To earn additional money we cut lawns, trimmed shrubs and cleaned flowerbeds for neighbors most weekdays during the summer. It was hard work, primarily because we were cutting grass using a hand mower. Since Dick had a special interest in flowers and would nurture them with great care, he would usually handle that part of our jobs. His attention to detail may have been why he had an uncanny ability to find four-leaf clovers. He found them everywhere!

One summer day, after Dick and I finished cutting Mrs. Gehrke's lawn for more than three hours, we returned home for lunch and told Mom we were thinking about raising our fee from $1.25 (for the both of us) to $1.50. She replied, "Absolutely not, she is a widow with four young children and can hardly afford to pay you $1.25." Needless to say we did not increase our fee.

Winter was our favorite time to earn money. We were able to earn three to four times as much by shoveling snow than we could by cutting grass, and it did not take as long. We developed a regular list of customers who would wait for us to shovel the snow from their sidewalks and driveways following every snowstorm.

Although Dick and I were not particularly handy and had little interest in things mechanical, we built an outdoor brick grill. The grill was functional, but poorly designed; it was utilized for only a few summers. We also built a rather poorly constructed rabbit hutch in an attempt to raise rabbits. We quickly concluded that rabbits were dirty and too prolific. It didn't take long for us to dismantle the hutch and move on to other things. We had a continuous quest to occupy and entertain ourselves.

One of our favorite summertime activities was visiting Carsonia Park, a local amusement park located on the present site of the Antietam Valley Recreational Center and pool in Pennside, Pennsylvania. The Bavarian Beer Garden, now Anthony's restaurant, was located near the entrance. Carsonia Park, operating each summer season from 1896 until 1950, featured many rides and attractions. Dick and I particularly enjoyed the Thunderbolt (a large roller coaster), Dodgem cars (battery-powered bumper cars), and the Old Mill (a ride in the dark in a gondola car through a moving channel of water, passing all sorts of scary scenes). We also frequented the Penny Arcade, the Ferris wheel and the musical carousel. We could keep ourselves amused for hours, only taking a break to eat lunch at one of the many picnic tables located throughout the park.

# 8

## Having a Good Time

DESPITE TIGHT BUDGETS AND MUCH SELF-SACRIFICE, Mom and Pop were able to find time to enjoy themselves. They would often go to the movies on Monday evenings. Mom was a bridge player and played with Aunt Claire and friends at the Reading Country Club on Tuesday afternoons. Every several years Mom and Pop would attend a formal Christmas dinner dance, also at the Reading Country Club. But the real fun was had when they went to New York City for a few days to attend Broadway shows. On those occasions, Dick and I and our siblings would remain home in the capable hands of Uncle Walter, who usually prepared our favorite meal, hot dogs and baked beans. When his meal was placed on the table we would substitute a rubber hot dog for his cooked one and anxiously wait for him to cut it. He always did so with great flourish, resulting in the rubber hot dog flying onto the floor and all of us erupting into laughter!

We also had fun when Aunt Peg visited from Shillington for the weekend. We would anxiously await her arrival at the 36th Street bus station across the street from our house. It was always special to have her stay overnight. Aunt Peg would play board and card games with us and allow the girls to comb her hair incessantly. She always expressed great interest in whatever we were doing. When Mom's brother John visited, he would also join in our activities; however he did not stay overnight. I remember Pop making sure Uncle John was on the 11:30 P.M. bus—the last bus leaving Reiffton.

Since our home had no air conditioning, on hot summer days we would frequently move the wicker furniture from the porch to the front yard under a large shade tree. Friends and family would gather there to relax and cool off. It was always a fun time, with great conversation among the adults and kids often lasting well into the evening.

On Friday nights in the 1930s and early 1940s, major boxing matches were frequently broadcast on the radio. Television would not become a household staple for another twenty years. Occasionally, Pop would invite some of our uncles and friends to the house to listen to big fights like the Max Schmeling vs. Joe Louis fight in 1938. As ten-year-olds, Dick and I were thrilled to be allowed to listen to the fights with the men. Our job was to bring food from the kitchen to the living room, where the radio was located. We were also the runners to bring fresh bottles of Sunshine beer to everyone when needed. Those evenings were special.

Uncle Walter frequently took us for rides in the countryside in his 1933 Plymouth Coupe. One of our favorite rides was sitting in the open rumble seat and going "over the three bridges." The bridges were located on Gibraltar Road, east of Reiffton, and culminated in the town of Gibraltar. We eagerly anticipated hearing and feeling the car rumble over the bridges' wooden slats.

Pop and Uncle Walter occasionally took Dick and me to the automobile races on a quarter-mile dirt racetrack at the Reading Fairgrounds near the present site of Boscov's North. The races were very popular at the time and were a major entertainment event. Several of the drivers were nationally known, including Tommy Hinnershitz from Oley, Pennsylvania, and Ted Horn, both of whom raced in the Indy 500. Horn never won the Indy 500 though his nine-straight top-four finishes at the Indianapolis Motor Speedway from 1936 to 1948 is a record that stands today.

For several years on Sunday afternoons during the late 1930s, Pop and Uncle Walter took Dick and me to watch the Reading Keys, a semipro football team. The games were played at the old Lauer's Park, at Third and Walnut Streets in Reading. One of the more notable teams the Keys played was the Philadelphia Eagles. They played competitively, but always lost to the Eagles by a few points. This was early in the history of professional football—certainly not the pro ball played today. My recollection is that Dick and I were more interested in the hot dogs, soda and candy vendors than the actual game.

Several times after the football games, Pop and Uncle Walter would visit a speakeasy in South Reading. Years before, the government had passed the Volstead Act, which made it illegal to manufacture or consume alcoholic beverages in the United States. Speakeasies were private establishments that served alcoholic drinks to admitted members. Since selling alcohol was illegal, members were advised to "speak easy" lest the police raid the establishment. Dick and I were perfectly content waiting in the car—Pop and Uncle Walter would bring us candy bars and soda—although I remember Mom not being very pleased.

During the summer of 1939, Mom, Pop, Mary, Dick and I attended the World's Fair at Flushing Meadows, New York. We stayed at the Hotel Piccadilly in the Theater District of New York City, fondly remembered for the cold water faucet in the bathroom—a first for Mary, Dick and me. I recall that we were frequently warned to stay away from the open windows without screens. The theme of the fair was the "world of tomorrow." It was the first international exposition to be futuristic in focus while continuing to promote cultural exchange among nations. How ironic given that World War II commenced shortly thereafter. The centerpiece buildings of the fair were the Trylon, a 700-foot high spire, and the Perisphere, a huge sphere that measured 180 feet in diameter. Inside the sphere was a giant depiction of the "world of tomorrow" with multiple highways, airplanes, vehicles, moving trains, villages and towns—simulating a huge train yard. Visitors were moved about within the sphere in self-propelled vehicles. Although the lines to enter the various country and commercial exhibits were long and very slow moving, we had a wonderful time. Visiting New York City for the first time was an added bonus.

On November 30, 1941, Pop took Dick and me to the Eagles vs. Chicago Bears game at Shibe Park, located at 21st Street and Lehigh Avenue in Philadelphia. The Bears—then the best team in the league—were the overwhelming favorite to defeat the Eagles. Led by legendary owner and coach George Halas, the Bears used a powerful new T-formation offense driven by Sid Luckman, the best passer in the game, and Ken Cavanaugh, a superior runner. At half time the Eagles were ahead 13 to 0, and we had high hopes for a big upset. In the second half, however, the Bears scored seven unanswered touchdowns and won the game easily, 49 to 13. It was a disappointing loss for the Eagles, but nonetheless exciting to watch the new T-formation offense executed by the best team in the National Football League.

Pop would occasionally take Dick and me on overnight fishing trips to Broomes Island, a small waterfront community on the Patuxent River in Maryland. Uncles Joe, John and Walter were sometimes with us as well. The fishing was always great fun. We usually fished for two days, returning late afternoon each day for a delicious meal. After Dick and I went to bed, the men played cards and enjoyed a few beers well into the night. We knew that to be the case since Dick and I would awaken early the next morning eager to go fishing, only to find the men still struggling to get out of bed.

When Dick and I were about twelve years old, Pop erected a basketball hoop in the backyard. We loved it—shooting hoops and playing one-on-one basketball for hours at a time. Pop broke a rib straining to erect the pole and wooden backboard, the only time he was injured during our youth. On one memorable occasion, a friend came over to play basketball and told us he had seen one of our younger sisters sitting on Perkiomen Avenue playing with her doll. Since Dick and I were the appointed babysitters at the time, we hustled over to get her. We were very fortunate that it was during wartime because there was little traffic on the highway!

One of the greatest gifts Mom and Pop gave us was a sense of humor. Teasing among siblings was the lifeblood of large families, and our family was no exception. Dick and I frequently teased our sisters—particularly Mary and Theresa—much to their annoyance and the displeasure and chagrin of Mom and Pop. For example, we would sit at the rectangular table in the kitchen for breakfast before school, with Dick and me on one side of the table facing Mary and Theresa. The pantry behind the girls contained a window. Dick or I would say, "Oh, look at that bird in the window!" The girls would inevitably turn around to look, only to realize we had teased them once more. Another example was our telling one of the girls that her skirt was large enough to fit around a house, and then placing it around a dollhouse. Obviously this was the beginning of our budding teasing natures!

# 9

# Brown's Cove

SUMMER VACATION EACH YEAR was a family trip to Brown's Cove near Baltimore. We stayed for several weeks in a cottage rented by Aunt Anna (Prendergast) and her friend Uncle Charlie, a retired B&O Railroad executive. Aunt Anna was Pop's first cousin (her mother was a sister of Pop's father) and had moved in with the Horrigan family at about the age of seven, following her mother's death. Aunt Anna assisted greatly in raising Uncle Walter, the youngest of Pop's four siblings. Following Pop's parents' deaths, Aunt Anna effectively became the matriarch of the family at the age of twenty-four.

The wooden-frame cottage at Brown's Cove was located under a large growth of shade trees at the top of a bank leading down to Back River, a tributary of the Chesapeake Bay. A long set of wooden stairs descended to a twenty-foot wharf. Farther into the river was an anchored raft from which we would jump and dive into the water for hours. The cottage had a large screened-in front porch, a living room, dining room, four bedrooms and a kitchen in the back of the house. There was no plumbing, therefore no inside bathroom nor running water. Just outside the kitchen door was a water pump and a large wooden icebox for soda and beer. At the rear of the backyard was a two-hole outhouse.

While Mom and the children remained at Brown's Cove for the two-week vacation, Pop would work during the week in Reading and join us only on weekends. As the sole proprietor of J. F. Horrigan Co., he never took a vacation. We would anxiously await his return on Friday evenings, and frequently ask if he could stay at least for several more days. It is clear in hindsight that Pop had no alternative given the economic conditions of the times. He had a large family to support and therefore work came first.

Aunt Anna seldom remained at Brown's Cove overnight while we were there; instead she would drive back in the evening to her home at 2632 East Baltimore Street in Baltimore, about twenty miles away. Aunt Anna was the organist at St. Elizabeth Church—a few steps from her home—and a part-time cashier at Hutzler's department store. Much to our delight, she would return to the cottage every several days with Berger cookies, our favorites, and many other treats.

Our younger cousins, Ann and Margaret Griffiths (Pop's sister Evelyn's daughters) and Lewis and Bobby Blakey (Pop's sister Myrtle's boys), would frequently join us at Brown's Cove. Our favorite place to go was Jerry's, a local grocery store and bar about a mile and a half away. When we were permitted to go to Jerry's, we would eat lunch, drink way too much soda and enjoy the player piano located in the hall adjacent to the bar.

Dick and I would frequently use the rowboat moored to the wharf at the cottage to fish and crab. We fished for stripers and white perch with our lightweight bamboo fishing poles, using a cork bobber and spreader with two hooks baited with either bloodworms or peeler crabs. Prior to crabbing, we would prepare a 200-yard long trotline of rope connected on each end to a buoy that was tied to another shorter rope and anchor. We put a piece of bait, usually tripe or eel, every several feet along the trotline. It was a lot of bait and a dirty smelly job! We would row out about a quarter of a mile and place the trotline into the water. Dick or I would then slowly raise the trotline. When the one pulling the line saw a crab nearing the surface of the water, the other would dip under the line with a long-handled net, scooping and dropping the crab into a large wooden basket. We would work the line several times resulting in many dozens of beautiful Chesapeake Bay blue crabs.

Aunt Anna steamed the crabs and then everyone would devour them at a newspaper-covered picnic table situated under a large shade tree next to the cottage. There was usually a keg of beer for the adults and bottles of soda kept cold in a wooden icebox for the children. Old family movies from that time clearly depicted the fun we all had.

The wooden icebox outside the back door of the cottage posed a problem for Mom because we would open the drinks using the bottle cap remover attached to the box and frequently drop the caps on the ground. One day Mom told everyone—children and adults alike—that whoever dropped a bottle cap on the ground would have to pick it up by his or her teeth. Tim and Ann Jaggers, close friends of Mom and Pop, were there at the time. Uncle Timmy immediately proceeded to open a bottle of soda and dropped the bottle cap to the ground. He then removed the bridge from his mouth and bent down using the false teeth in his hand to pick up the bottle cap, to the laughter of all assembled. Whether it was a spontaneous act or planned by Uncle Timmy and Mom, it certainly made an impression on all of us.

During the summer of 1940, Uncle Walter was diagnosed with diverticulitis, requiring what was considered at the time to be major surgery. Having changed jobs the previous year, Uncle Walter was then a police officer for the B&O Railroad in Zanesville, Ohio. The surgery took place in Baltimore, and he planned to recuperate for six weeks at Brown's Cove. Dick and I, eleven years old at the time, were invited to stay with Uncle Walter since he could not be alone. Aunt Anna would arrive every several days with provisions, but Uncle Walter, Dick and I were usually alone. Other guests would arrive for the weekends, but our favorite times were when only the three of us were there. We learned many card games, listened to innumerable stories, enjoyed Uncle Walter's display of magic, fished, crabbed, swam, cut the grass and walked to Jerry's for supplies when needed.

One of Uncle Walter's creative games was for us to make up as many names as possible for the two-holed wooden green outhouse at the end of the yard behind the cottage. Among the names I recall were "the hockey poo hamper," "the little green house in the rear," "the two-holer" and "Conshohocken." The latter name originated from the fact that Uncle Timmy worked at Lee Tires in Conshohocken, and there was a Lee Tire sign in front of the outhouse.

One of Uncle Walter's responsibilities as a B&O Railroad police officer was to routinely patrol the rail yards. He told us about a B&O rail worker named J. B. King who would write his name on all the boxcars after inspecting them to certify that they had been appropriately locked and secured. Uncle Walter then recited a ditty scribed on many of the cars: "Who be this man J. B. King whose name I see on everything? Be he poor or be he rich, he sure is a prominent son of a bitch."

The six weeks with Uncle Walter at Brown's Cove during the summer of 1940 still resonate as the most fun-filled and memorable extended vacation Dick and I ever experienced as youngsters.

# 10

# A Brother in All but Name

MOM'S OLDER SISTER ESTHER AND HER HUSBAND, Joe Cunningham, lived in Los Angeles with their four children: Joe, Jack, Joan and Jerry. Jerry, the same age as Dick and me, came to Reading with Aunt Esther for a visit during the summer of 1941. We were excited to have him join us for our vacation at Brown's Cove. We had a great two weeks, spending most of the time swimming and fishing.

Uncle Joe died on April 3, 1943, while Joe and Jack were in the Coast Guard and Joan was away at college. Aunt Esther and Jerry returned to Reading in late summer that year and lived at our grandmother's house in Shillington for about a year and a half. Jerry spent the majority of time at our home and became like another brother to Dick and me.

Jerry, Dick and I were classmates during our sophomore year at Central Catholic High School. As fifteen-year-old boys, we had many common interests and spent most of our time together. Jerry again joined us for our summer vacation at Brown's Cove in 1944.

A memorable activity for the three of us was attending

the Reading Brooks minor league baseball games at Lauer's Park. The Brooks was a farm team for the Brooklyn Dodgers. Carl Furillo, a nineteen-year-old from Stony Creek Mills in Exeter Township, was the star of the team. Known as "The Reading Rifle," Furillo could throw base runners out at home by throwing the ball from left field to home plate without the ball ever hitting the ground. Furillo subsequently enjoyed a successful career as a right fielder in the major leagues for the Brooklyn Dodgers and later the Los Angeles Dodgers.

Another player on the Reading Brooks was the infamous Al Campanis who subsequently had a brief career as a second baseman with the Brooklyn Dodgers. Campanis became general manager of the Los Angeles Dodgers from 1968 to 1987. He was fired in 1987 because of controversial remarks he made regarding blacks in baseball during an interview with Ted Koppel on *Nightline.*

# 11

## Our Love of Baseball

DICK AND I FOLLOWED THE AMERICAN LEAGUE PHILADELPHIA A'S and the National League Philadelphia Phillies on the radio every day during the season. The A's home games were announced live from Shibe Park, later named Connie Mack Stadium. The Phillies home games were also announced live, first from Baker Bowl at North 15th and West Huntingdon Streets and later from the larger Shibe Park. The away games were transmitted via ticker tape from the site of the game back to the radio studio. Each play was then reconstructed and announced as if it were live to the radio audience. You could hear the ticker in the background as the announcers, Claude Haring and By Saam, recreated each play. We felt like we were behind home plate at the ballpark.

While in grade school and junior high, Dick and I played a baseball board game for hours on our front porch. We created a league of teams similar to the number of major league teams, kept score of each game and calculated batting averages and league standings. We couldn't wait for Pop to come home after work to ask us how each of the teams was doing, which team was in first place and who had the highest batting averages. What patience, imagination and love of baseball it took for us to detail all the action.

Dick and I would play catch by the hour during baseball season and frequently played ball with several of our neighborhood friends on the field behind the Reiffton Grade School. If there were only three of us we played "one out goes out," with each of us rotating as the pitcher, the batter and the fielder. We always created a game no matter how many players were available. Baseball at that time was truly America's Game.

On June 28, 1939, Pop, Dick and I attended a daytime doubleheader between the Philadelphia A's and the New York Yankees at Shibe Park in Philadelphia. (See Appendix, pp. 102–103.) The games were memorable for two reasons. First, the Yankees set a record for home runs by one team in a doubleheader—eight in the first game and five in the second. When the thirteenth home run was hit late in the second game, we told Pop that a new record for home runs in a doubleheader had been set. A few moments later the public address announcer said the same thing, an indication of how closely Dick and I had followed baseball and baseball statistics. The second memorable event was that Lou Gehrig, having announced his retirement several weeks earlier due to his declining health, presented the Yankee lineup to the umpires before the first game and received a standing ovation from the crowd. Two years later, Gehrig died from ALS, subsequently referred to as "Lou Gehrig's Disease." Gehrig held the major league record for playing the most consecutive games (2,130), with his last game played on April 30, 1939. It wasn't until 1995 that Baltimore Orioles' Cal Ripken Jr. broke Gehrig's consecutive game record.

Another fond memory was on Sunday, September 28, 1941, when the Boston Red Sox played a doubleheader in Philadelphia. Ted Williams, concluding his third season as left fielder for the Red Sox, had a batting average of .400 going into the doubleheader, the final two games of the season. There had been speculation he might sit out the games to preserve his .400 average. That afternoon, Dick and I attended a cowboy movie at the Warner Theater in Reading and when Pop picked us up afterwards, we asked if Williams played and how he did. Pop told us he had played both games, and went 6 for 8 to finish the season with a .406 batting average; no major league player has hit .400 for a full season since then. Following that season, Williams interrupted his baseball career for three years to serve in the military during World War II.

# 12

## Holiday Traditions

ON THANKSGIVING DAY MORNINGS, Pop would take as many of the children old enough to do so on long walks through the fields and streams behind our house. We really looked forward to the walks and spending time with Pop. He always stuffed toilet paper in his pocket for any emergencies. No doubt having most of the children out of the house for several hours in the morning was a great help for Mom. We certainly loved the smell of the turkey cooking in the oven when we returned home.

Christmas was a big holiday for our family. There was always a Christmas Eve party at our grandmother's home. After a big dinner prepared by Aunt Claire we would move to the living room where Aunt Peg, acting as Santa Claus, distributed the presents from under the Christmas tree. Another fond memory of the Christmas Eve party—actually any time we visited our grandmother's home—was Aunt Hilda's fully stocked drawer of candy in the dining room. Several generations of our family fondly remember Aunt Hilda as the "candy lady."

Mom and Pop would decorate our tree on Christmas Eve after all the children had gone to bed. They would lay the Christmas presents out in separate piles for each of us. Pop would often set up a train yard. Neither of them could have had much sleep on those nights! We attended Christmas Mass in the morning after opening the presents and couldn't wait to get back to them after Mass. Frequently, Aunt Anna and Uncle Charlie would arrive in the afternoon for another round of presents followed by a big turkey dinner. Uncle Charlie always carved the turkey whenever he and Aunt Anna visited.

One Christmas, when we were eleven years old, Mary, Dick and I received new blue Rollfast bicycles. They had big balloon tires, no gears or hand brakes and were very heavy to ride. They were the only full sized two-wheelers we ever had and we loved them. Dick and I rode the bikes throughout Reiffton and back and forth to Mt. Penn for years—our transportation to baseball practice, baseball games and many other activities.

Easter was also a memorable time of year. Our family attended Mass on Holy Thursday and church services on Good Friday. Dick and I anxiously awaited the conclusion of Lent at noon on Holy Saturday to resume eating candy, which we had often given up as our Lenten sacrifice. Early Easter morning, we hunted for our baskets and frequently compared the amount of candy each of us had received. Following Easter Sunday Mass, many relatives would join the family for Mom's delicious ham dinner.

# 13

## Our Daily Routine

Dick and I were similar in our likes and dislikes. We were truly best friends, with common skills, interests and aptitudes. We were good students, with very similar marks through grade school, high school and college. We were content being alone together, even though we enjoyed the friendship of our neighborhood buddies and schoolmates.

For seventh and eighth grades Dick and I attended Exeter Junior High School, located on the Boyertown Pike in Jacksonwald. We boarded a school bus each morning at Reiffton Grade School for the drive through St. Lawrence. There was an old one-room schoolhouse on the grounds of the school where Dick and I attended health class. The schoolhouse is still there today and is considered a historic building.

We were fortunate to have several excellent junior high school teachers; the most memorable were Mr. Rhoads and Mr. Hopkins, who taught history and civics, respectively. After classes Dick and I frequently talked with them about the subject matters of the day and their application to current events. They were good teachers, skilled in ways to challenge and excite students. For example, Dick and I had seen the movie *Mr. Smith Goes to Washington* at the Majestic Theater in Mt. Penn and discussed it after civics class with Mr. Hopkins. He talked about politics and how accurately the movie depicted real political life. Dick and I became fascinated with the subject—an interest sustained thereafter. After history class one day, Mr. Rhoads encouraged us to remain focused on our studies since we were good students with a high probability of attending college.

Both men subsequently entered the service during World War II. We were sad to hear that Mr. Rhoads was severely injured during the war. Mr. Hopkins was fortunate to return home safely and attempted to enter politics by running unsuccessfully for a Pennsylvania House legislative seat.

After school Dick and I were always outside playing ball, climbing the rocks or enjoying other outdoor activities. We would usually come home at about 4:00 P.M., lie on the floor, and listen to a series of fifteen-minute radio shows such as *Dick Tracy, Terry and the Pirates, Tarzan of the Apes, Jack Armstrong* and *The Shadow.* Occasionally after dinner we would also listen to radio shows such as *Fibber McGee and Molly, George Burns and Gracie Allen, Amos and Andy, Jack Benny* and *Lux Radio Theatre.* Listening to these shows, which seemed quite real, strongly enhanced our imaginations.

One of our neighborhood friends, Buck Weidenhammer, lived on a farm two blocks from our home, on what is now 38th Street in Reiffton. We would visit Buck, exploring the out buildings and crawling throughout the barn. On one occasion in the barn, Buck, Dick and I started a fire to grill hot dogs. Fortunately for us his Dad saw what we were doing. He extinguished the fire and told us to never attempt it again.

Dick and I frequently played ping-pong in the basement

of our home. Occasionally our desire to win resulted in the loser slamming the paddle against the edge of the table and denting the table. When Pop discovered what we had been doing he took the paddles from us for a period of time. This occurred more than once and finally after receiving a stern warning—no more slamming the paddles or they will be taken away for good—we obeyed.

Dick and I would often imitate a football game by sitting on the inside edges of our twin beds facing each other. One of us was the ball carrier and the other the defender, trying to prevent the ball carrier from reaching the end zone, i.e., the other side of the defender's bed. The ensuing clash and shoving frequently resulted in the beds sliding across the floor, creating much noise and clamor heard throughout the house. The football games finally stopped after several strong admonitions to do so. Although Mom and Pop understood the normal instincts of brothers to tussle from time to time, they had the sense to know when enough was enough and firmly acted accordingly.

The only time I recall Pop displaying real anger was when Dick and I were building a shed adjacent to the side of the house. We inadvertently left a plank of wood on the ground with an exposed upright nail. Clara, the nanny living with us at the time, walked into the yard and stepped on the nail, requiring Pop to take her to the hospital for treatment. Unfortunately Mom was about to discharge Clara and the accident extended her stay for several more weeks. We learned later about the pending discharge and fully understood Pop's anger and frustration at the time of the accident.

Dick and I followed the behavioral standards set quietly by Mom and Pop, not out of fear of being punished but rather from the desire not to disappoint them. Interestingly, as adults our siblings have expressed similar sentiments.

At our home at 3601 Perkiomen Avenue, there was a large dinner bell affixed to the top of a wooden pole in the yard near the entrance to the back porch. Mom would ring the bell signaling that it was time to come home for dinner. No matter where we were in Reiffton, Dick and I would hear the bell and come right home.

Dinner with the entire family was very important. It was the time for our family to be together and discuss events of the day and each of our personal experiences. Mom sat at the head of the table closest to the kitchen, while Pop sat at the opposite end. Dick and I usually sat to Pop's right and the girls sat to his left. Sometimes Pop would play numbers games with us like "buzz." The object of the game was to say buzz whenever the number seven, or a number divisible by seven, came up as we sequentially counted aloud around the table. Another game Pop often played was to give us a number and subsequent instructions—whether to add, subtract, divide or multiply other numbers—and see if we knew the correct answer when he asked for it. As a result, we all became very comfortable with numbers and math.

Another dining room table lesson was the introduction of two principles of good conversation: First, never say something that does not meet at least two of the following criteria—is it kind, is it necessary, is it true? Second, the best subjects for worthwhile conversation are in this order—about ideas, places and lastly about people. These principles remained with Dick and me all our lives.

After dinner the older children had certain tasks. Dick and I would help Mom with the dishes and Mary and Theresa would help the younger girls with their baths before bedtime, or vice versa. Dick and I also had two chores to do every day in the basement. One was to check the salt level of the water softener and add salt as needed; the other was to shovel coal into a hopper connected to the coal-fired heater. Mom was very well organized and taught all of us how to complete our chores efficiently and in a timely manner.

# 14

# St. Catharine's Athletics

ALTHOUGH STILL IN PUBLIC SCHOOL while in eighth grade, Dick and I played on St. Catharine's Catholic Youth Organization (CYO) team in the Catholic Grade School Basketball League. All games were played on Saturday mornings in the new Central Catholic High School gymnasium. We played on the league all-star team against the championship St. Joseph's CYO team. We became friends with all the players in the league, many of whom became classmates at Central the following year.

In the spring of 1941, Father William Faunce, a newly ordained priest who ultimately became a close family friend, was assigned to St. Catharine's. One Sunday, Father invited parish boys interested in forming a baseball team to meet him in the sacristy after Mass. Dick and I expressed interest, along with our friends Tom Powers and Bob Didyoung, and this was the beginning of St. Catharine's baseball team. Tom's dad, George Powers, was our coach. Pop and other fathers provided the transportation when necessary. We played ball every summer until Dick and I graduated from high school. Initially we created a ball field at the present site of the Mt. Penn A Field on High Street. Home plate at that time was in centerfield of the present A Field. It was a rough field, suitable only for inter-team and practice games. The only equipment provided initially by St. Catharine's was the base bags. We used our own bats and balls. As the team progressed, full uniforms, balls and bats were supplied.

During our first practice game, we played rather poorly, and Father Faunce threatened to take the base bags and go home—an incident we always chided him about. Although Father could become quite irascible, he truly respected all the kids and deserves credit for beginning what became a tradition of very successful St. Catharine's baseball teams. The city of Reading had an excellent recreational baseball program, as there was no organized Little League Baseball at the time. The first year St. Catharine's played in the Reading C-league and won the championship; in the second year we played in the B-league and again won the championship. We then moved to the A-league and did well but never won the title—it was a much stronger league with better, more seasoned ball players.

Dick was a very good catcher who could throw out runners at second from a crouch behind home plate. His catcher's mitt was small and sparsely padded by today's standards, resulting in Dick's left hand being almost twice as thick as his right hand by the end of the season. I was a good fielder with a strong arm, playing either third or second base. We were only average hitters.

Games were played at numerous Reading ball fields including Pendora Park, Egelman's Park, Schlegel Park, Hillside Park, 11th and Pike, Baer Park and Oakbrook. Following games at Pendora Park, Dick and I would often stop at Bielski's, 19th Street and Perkiomen Avenue, for a taste of their delicious draft root beer. Our favorite place to go in Mt. Penn after games and practices was Heberlings, a local store at 25th and Cumberland Streets. We played pinball, enjoyed bottles of soda and frequently sat outside with our teammates, visiting for another hour or more. Those small gatherings were enjoyed as much as the games, particularly if we had won.

The best pitcher on the team was Joe Reedy, a lefty, who was also a high school classmate. One evening while playing at Baer Park in the City B-League, Joe pitched a no-hitter. Dick was behind the plate and I was playing third base. Joe had a very good fastball, good control, and an incredible slider—then called a drop—with the pitch literally dropping about two feet as it crossed the plate. He had many strikeouts and the remaining outs were weak infield grounders. While Dick had to work hard catching Joe's drops, we fielders had it much easier simply watching—quite a pitching effort!

After several seasons, Joe joined the Reading area's only American Legion team at that time, the Keys, for whom the best teenage players in the area were invited to play. In July 1946 the Reading Keys played Coplay—a small town near Allentown, Pennsylvania—for a berth in the State Legion playoffs. Dick and I attended the game at Pendora Park with more than 5,000 other fans—an amazingly large crowd for a Legion game played at an open public athletic field. The reason for the large attendance was because Joe was pitching for the Keys against Coplay's Curt Simmons, who later became a star pitcher for the Philadelphia Phillies. Coplay won the game 5 to 3 although Joe gave up only three hits. By then, Simmons was well on his way to becoming a major league pitcher.

Our St. Catharine's team also played several games against St. Elizabeth's baseball team in Baltimore. (This is the parish we would later become part of when living with Aunt Anna during our years at Loyola College.) The team stayed at Brown's Cove and enjoyed the water as much as playing baseball. Aunt Anna made the best fried chicken and supplied all the treats that a group of hungry teenagers would enjoy. We drove to Baltimore each day for a game and returned afterwards to Brown's Cove for more food and fun. It was a great experience for everyone and for some team-mates, the first time they had ever traveled outside of Reading. We played four games over two summers and fin-ished 1 and 3 against St. Elizabeth's. They were the better team, and their star pitcher was one of the best eigh-teen-year-old pitchers in the Baltimore area at the time. One of the St. Elizabeth's players, George Frantz, was also a catcher; he later played baseball at Loyola during our fi-nal year of college.

# 15

# Central Catholic High School

THE NEXT REAL TRANSITION IN OUR LIVES was attending Central Catholic High School. The school had opened just two years prior to Dick and me starting ninth grade in 1942. Father Charles Allwein was the principal, and Father Raymond Leichner was the assistant principal and athletic director. Sister Casimer, an icon at Central having taught there for more than thirty years, was our physics teacher. Our favorite teacher was Sister Rosanna, who taught us many math courses. She was a no-nonsense disciplinarian and excellent teacher. Our love of math, having begun with Pop's playing numbers games with us as children, was enhanced by Sister Rosanna and continued for the rest of our lives.

We enjoyed everything about high school—the activities, the sports, our classmates and our studies. Dick and I pursued the college prep track and were on the honor roll every semester. Our grades were almost identical throughout the four years. (See Appendix, pp. 104–107.)

Pop would usually drive Dick and me to school on his way to work and we generally returned home by public transportation. During our senior year, our new basketball coach, Joe Schaaf, would drop us off after basketball practice on his way home to Limerick, Pennsylvania. Another means of transportation was hitchhiking, which did not have the social stigma that it does today. On April 12, 1945, during a bus strike, Dick and I hitchhiked home after school. The driver picked us up on Mineral Spring Road near school and told us that President Roosevelt had died shortly before at his summer home in Warm Springs, Georgia. It was tragic news and a great shock. Dick and I were sixteen years old and he was the only president we had ever known, having been in office slightly more than twelve years. President Roosevelt had led the country through the Depression, inspired confidence in a country beaten down with massive crop failures and business implosions and had nearly seen us through to complete victory in World War II.* Everyone alive at that time remembers where he or she had been when President Roosevelt died—no doubt similar to the memory of President John F. Kennedy's assassination in 1963.

A funny incident during the summer of 1945 involved our sister Mary and our high school buddy, Jimmy Gallen. The four of us walked to the Reiffton Fire Company for ice cream. To raise additional funds, the fire company sold Dolly Madison ice cream and other snacks at a counter on the first floor of the fire station. As we approached the counter, Jimmy said to the clerk, "Do you know that these three are triplets?" The clerk responded that he could see the resemblance between Mary and Dick but didn't see me as looking like either of them. Jimmy always kept us laughing and ultimately became a lifelong friend.

---

* Given President Roosevelt's poor health at the time of his reelection for a fourth term in November 1944, Congress passed the 22nd Amendment to the Constitution on March 21, 1947, limiting future presidents to two terms. The requisite number of states ratified the Amendment on February 27, 1951.

Dick and I were co-managers of the school's football team in our senior year. Our responsibilities included tracking all the equipment and coordinating activities for the school administrators, coaches and players. While at preseason football camp in late summer 1945 we also helped prepare meals and did sundry other tasks necessary to support forty football players, several priests and a relatively new coaching staff. We had a great time at camp, playing cards in the evening and simply enjoying the experience of being away from home for the week with our friends. As co-managers of the team, Dick and I learned a lot about responsibility, organizational behavior and how to get things done efficiently.

Dick and I played basketball all four years at Central Catholic. We had a lot of playing time on the freshmen and junior varsity teams. Our varsity team was very good, and we were satisfied to be on the second team pushing the starters during practice, though we saw limited game action. Too bad our basketball skills peaked in grade school, when named to the all-star CYO team, rather than in high school!

Our team had an excellent record every year and won the Williamsport Catholic High School Invitational tournament in our junior and senior years. Catholic schools at that time did not participate in the State PIAA championship playoffs.

Varsity baseball at Central Catholic had its inaugural season in 1945. Dick and I played on the team in both our junior and senior years. Dick continued his baseball career as a catcher and I as a third baseman. We had good teams, but never played more than ten games a year. The seasons were much too short.

At the conclusion of our senior season in 1946, our baseball team was invited to the Jesuit novitiate in Wernersville, Pennsylvania, to play against the Jesuit seminarians. At that time there were about 150 young men in the seminary in various stages of training to become priests. After the game we had lunch with the seminarians against whom we had played. Two of them befriended Dick and me, knowing that we were interested in attending Loyola College, a Jesuit institution. We corresponded with them for about a year and later learned they had dropped out of the seminary. That day at the novitiate was a great experience and a good introduction to the learning environment of a Jesuit institution, as we contemplated the possibility of attending Loyola in the fall.

On June 9, 1946, Dick and I graduated from Central Catholic. Our commencement ceremony was held at St. Paul's Church in Reading. (See Appendix, pp. 108–109.) We graduated among the top ten in our class of 115 students. Dick was given the Most Cooperative Student Award related to his high scholastic achievements and all-around support of school activities. I won the Latin Award for having the highest aggregate marks for four years of Latin. Truth be told, there were only five of us who took four years of Latin!

# 16

# Heading Off to Loyola College

IN MAY OF 1946, Dick and I were given an entrance exam at Loyola College in Baltimore, with about sixty other prospective students. There were no SATs or other standardized tests at the time; therefore admission to Loyola was based solely on our high school records and successfully passing the entrance exam. We were thrilled to receive notice several weeks later indicating that we had been accepted as freshmen to begin in the fall of 1946.

Loyola was an all-male college with no dormitories or other housing alternatives so all students were "day hops." At the time, all undergraduate programs at Loyola were for three years, which included a two-month summer semester each year. The purpose of accelerating the undergraduate program was to accommodate the large number of veterans attending Loyola under the G.I. Bill. After World War II, Congress passed the G.I. Bill to recognize and reward those service men and women who, upon being discharged, were inclined to pursue a college degree. The bill entitled the veterans to attend college with a substantial subsidy from the federal government. The accelerated three-year college curriculum facilitated their return to civilian life as productive members of the workforce. The G.I. Bill was no doubt the best piece of federal legislation ever passed to positively affect education in the United States.

Our attending Loyola at that time created a substantial financial burden for Mom and Pop. In the years following the end of World War II, the U.S. auto industry was just beginning to convert from the production of military vehicles to the production of automobiles. As a result, there had been few cars for Pop to finance during the previous four or five years—hence little income.

Loyola was our school of choice for several reasons—Pop graduated from Loyola High School and Dick and I were able to save money by living with Aunt Anna. Every several weeks Pop sent both Dick and me $10 for personal expenses. We augmented our income by tutoring and correcting "blue book" exams at Loyola and by working at the Baltimore Post Office during the Christmas season.

In 1916 Pop had turned down a full scholarship to Loyola College, choosing alternatively to enlist in the Army during World War I. It was a decision he regretted for the rest of his life. He fully understood the value of higher education and was determined that all his children have the opportunity to attend college. Dick and I were the first to do so even though financial resources at the time were very limited.

Dick and I were eager to begin school in the fall and were pleased to know our home-away-from-home would be with Aunt Anna. Her house was a typical Baltimore three-story row home with marble front steps, located across the street from Patterson Park. The first floor included a living room, dining room, kitchen and back porch. Aunt Anna's bedroom and another bedroom and bath were on the second floor of the house. Our bedroom, bath and study were on the third floor. Our accommodations were comfortable, quiet and conducive to studying. Aunt Anna prepared sandwiches for our lunch at school and we ate most of our other meals with her at home.

Dick and I quickly adjusted to the urban environment of a big city, influenced substantially by our living in St. Elizabeth Parish. Aunt Anna's home was only a few doors away from the rectory and the church. The pastor of the parish was Monsignor Jerome Sebastian.* He and his assistant pastors—Fathers Childress, Eccles and McGrain—were most welcoming to Dick and me. They introduced us to many young parishioners and invited us to parish activities that included monthly dances in the parish hall.

Dick and I would occasionally join Aunt Anna in the choir loft at St. Elizabeth's when she was playing the organ. She was an excellent organist, and we loved watching her play. Aunt Anna also played for innumerable weddings—as many as six or seven on a Saturday—since so many young men had recently returned from the service and were getting married. Although Aunt Anna had a backup organist—a nun who taught music at St. Elizabeth Grade School—she never wanted to disappoint the couple by asking Sister to substitute for her.

Soon after we moved in with Aunt Anna, Uncle Charlie suggested that since Dick and I were living with her, he could now move into one of the spare bedrooms in the house. She told us, "If Charlie ever suggests you talk to me

---

* Although remaining in residence at St. Elizabeth Parish, Monsignor Sebastian was appointed auxiliary bishop of Baltimore in 1953. Coincidentally, Dick and I saw the bishop in Baltimore in February 1958 when he offered the invocation prior to a Loyola-sponsored dinner honoring Massachusetts senator John F. Kennedy. By that time, Senator Kennedy had launched his campaign to become president in the forthcoming 1960 election. We were struck by how young he looked and also very impressed by his speaking style. Dick and I saw Senator Kennedy again in the fall of 1959 during his presidential campaign stop at Fifth and Penn Streets in Reading.

about his leaving the Knights of Columbus apartments and moving in with us, tell him no. I am happy to have him here for dinner every night but that is enough."

We generally boarded the crosstown bus several blocks from the house and proceeded directly to Loyola College at North Charles Street and Cold Spring Lane. It was about a thirty-minute bus ride. Sometimes our cousins Anne and Margaret would board the same bus en route to Seton Girls High School. Our school days were spent in classrooms, the library, the cafeteria, the gymnasium or on the baseball field. We frequently played cards in the cafeteria or studied between classes before returning home by bus. This became an everyday routine unless someone had a car or if we were practicing or playing intercollegiate baseball and Uncle Charlie was there to drive us home.

Dick and I attended as many school activities as possible, including plays, lectures, dances, and basketball and lacrosse games. We made many good friends along the way. We also enjoyed going to the movies at the neighborhood Belnord Theater where first-rate films were shown. Many times we would catch a movie at the Belnord the night before exams since we were usually well prepared at that point.

On summer nights Dick and I would sit on Aunt Anna's marble steps in front of the house and listen to the Baltimore Orioles baseball games on the radio. At that time the Orioles played in the AAA International League and always had a good team. Aunt Anna and her neighbor Robert Ritaliata, a local district justice known as Judge, would frequently join us for the games while sharing snacks and a few bottles of National Bohemian beer. It was at that time that Dick and I learned to enjoy beer. Judge Ritaliata was a very interesting man who enjoyed talking about current events and telling stories about Baltimore in the days when Pop lived there.

In the spring of our first year at Loyola, Dick and I made the varsity baseball team. We were not first-string players, but played in most games, competing with teams from Catholic University, Western Maryland, Towson State, LaSalle, St. Joseph's, Gallaudet, Washington College and Mount St. Mary's, among others. Our team was very good, having won the Mason Dixon Conference baseball championship in 1947. In 1948 we lost to Randolph Macon in the final playoff game. Uncle Charlie attended most of our practices and home games. Emil "Lefty" Reitz was our baseball coach, as well as the basketball coach and college athletic director. Coincidentally, Lefty had pitched for Villanova and his catcher was John Krajsa, who subsequently owned a consumer finance company in Allentown. About five years later I met John through the Pennsylvania Financial Services Association, and we became close friends.

The most memorable and toughest day was in the spring of 1947 when Dick was beaned in the head by a pitch during an inter-team practice game. As there were no batting helmets in those days, Dick sustained the full force of a fastball thrown by our very strong right-handed pitcher, Sid Roche. I was playing third base and saw Dick crumble to the ground. The game quickly came to a halt as we all rushed to Dick's aid. A very large lump immediately developed on his left temple. Fortunately Uncle Charlie was there and rushed us to the hospital. Dick was diagnosed and treated for a severe brain concussion. He remained in the hospital for several days and fully recovered from the concussion. Notwithstanding that experience, Dick finished the season with the team and enjoyed it very much.

Dick and I also played basketball on St. Elizabeth's adult basketball team during our years at Loyola. Practices were held in the parish hall and games were played in a public school gymnasium about ten blocks away on the other side of Patterson Park. We had a good team and won the majority of our games; Dick and I were the team's high scorers. After one of the games, Ernie Orlando, a referee, asked if we were the Horrigan boys from Reading. A native of Reading, he worked during the week in Baltimore. Occasionally Mr. Orlando invited us to join him on his weekend trips back home, which we greatly appreciated. The deal was that we would pay for the gas. Fortunately he was very conservative in his consumption of gas, driving at moderate speeds and turning off the engine and coasting down several very long hills on Route 10 near Morgantown, Pennsylvania. He was a good man and very thoughtful. After his having driven us home the first time we never again challenged Mr. Orlando's calls on the basketball court.

# 17

# Loyola Memories

MARCH 14, 1947, WAS A BIG DAY for the Horrigan family. Dick and I were having dinner with Aunt Anna that Friday evening when Pop called to tell us that our brother Mike was born. We came home within the next several days and were excited to visit Mom and Mike in the hospital. With his wry sense of humor Pop remarked that since most of the fathers visiting their wives in maternity were young veterans, Dick and I would look more like Mike's father than he.

In August of 1948, following our second year at Loyola, Dick and I were invited to play for a local Reading sandlot baseball team. August was the only month we were home from college other than holidays, so it was great to be home without studies and a bonus to play ball during the break. The AMVETS, a local veterans club organized after World War II, sponsored our team. The AMVETS clubhouse was located on the south side of Penn Street near the Penn Street Bridge. After the games we would return to the clubhouse for free beer, an added bonus.

Our good friend Jimmy Gallen was also home from

Villanova during this time and Dick and I spent a lot of time with him. One day Aunt Hilda, who worked in the Berks County District Attorney's office, called to warn us not to go to the bar in Angelica Store on Route 625 in Cumru Township that evening because it was going to be raided. She said rather sternly since we were underage, "If you are there when the bar is raided, do not expect any help from me!" Needless to say, Jimmy, Dick and I found other bars that served minors that night. Thank you, Aunt Hilda!

During our final year in college, Pop gave us a 1936 Plymouth to commute back and forth to Reading. It was an old, rather dilapidated car that burned gallons of oil. We kept a case of oil in the trunk and would stop every twenty miles to replace the burned oil. It was our first car and provided a welcome modicum of independence. We knew it was a heap since Pop paid only $125 for it. A humorous incident was when Uncle Charlie gave Dick and me his Cadillac one evening to attend a Loyola school dance. Aunt Anna drove Uncle Charlie in our car back to his apartment in downtown Baltimore. It was raining that evening and our car had a leaky roof. Without missing a beat, Aunt Anna opened an umbrella inside the car and calmly drove Uncle Charlie home. Aunt Anna was unflappable!

While at Loyola we spent a considerable amount of time at Brown's Cove playing cards and enjoying the water with our college friends. It was a wonderful place to relax and a great diversion from school. Aunt Anna was there occasionally, although most of the time we were there alone. There were chores to be done, including grass cutting, trimming the shrubs around the cottage, keeping the grounds free of leaves and debris, cleaning the outhouse and painting several of the rooms in the spring. Aunt Anna liked bright-colored rooms to match all the multicolored Fiesta dishes she had in the dining room cabinet. We were pleased to be there and had no problem handling the chores.

During our last year at Loyola, Dick and I organized,

captained and played on a college intramural basketball team known as the Keystoners. Having won the college intramural league championship, the Keystoners were invited to play a faculty team, comprised mostly of Jesuits, preliminary to the NAIA Championship basketball game between the Loyola varsity team and Texas Wesleyan. The Championship game, played in Kansas City and teletyped back to Loyola, was reconstructed and announced live by our classmate Vince Bagley. Vince went on to become a leading sports announcer for NBC in Baltimore. Even though the Keystoners and Loyola both lost, we greatly enjoyed playing before a full gymnasium of fans that evening. A possible factor contributing to the Keystoners' loss was that Dick and I and several teammates had dinner and a few beers beforehand at Andy's Bar and Grill. One of our teammates, who likely had had too much to drink, was thrown out of the game following an altercation with a player on the faculty team—Father Arthur, dean of discipline!

In March of 1949, Dick and I and several college friends watched the National Invitational Tournament Championship basketball game in New York City between Loyola University of Chicago and San Francisco University on a small black-and-white television set in Aunt Anna's living room. Loyola was an all-black team—the first all-black basketball team we had ever seen. We were all rooting for Loyola to win, but they unfortunately lost by one point, 48 to 47.

During our time in Baltimore, we occasionally visited with Aunt Evelyn, Uncle Garrett and our cousins Ann and Margaret, who lived several blocks away. One evening, when Dick and I arrived home from school, Aunt Evelyn and the girls were there with Aunt Anna and were visibly distraught. We learned that Uncle Garrett had died earlier that day. It was a sad experience for all. We saw a lot more of Aunt Evelyn and the girls thereafter.

The first semester of our freshman year was by far the most difficult until we learned how to better utilize our time, study more efficiently, take better notes and adjust to the faster pace of college courses and professors. Business subjects included accounting, economics, insurance, economics of money and banking, executive management, business law, government and business, marketing and business organization. Liberal arts courses included Spanish, English, ethics, history, natural theology, psychology, sociology, religion, epistemology, ontology, cosmology, logic and philosophy. All of our business professors were laymen, with both business and teaching experience. Jesuit professors taught our religion and philosophy classes. We enjoyed all our classes with the exception of Spanish, which was never a favorite.

Particularly noteworthy was our freshman religion professor Father William Herlihy. On the first day of class, Father asked each of the approximately seventy-five students for his name and requested that we sit in the same seats thereafter. By our next class, and every class following, Father called on each of us by name. Not only did he have a remarkable memory, he was also an excellent professor who made the study of religion come alive. As a testament to Father Herlihy's thoughtful nature, during the summer before our third year at Loyola, he stopped to visit Dick and me in Reiffton while en route to visit family in New York City.

Our second-year religion professor, Father Joseph d'Invilliers, was also excellent. He had been academic dean the previous year and had registered us for classes. Rank was clearly meaningless among the Jesuits, as one year Father was the dean and the following year he was teaching religion classes. Father retired to the Jesuit novitiate in Wernersville many years later.

One of our most interesting and challenging professors was Father Thomas Higgins. Father taught us logic, ethics and many philosophy courses. We utilized the textbook he had authored, which was also used in many other Jesuit colleges. His classes were very interesting and provocative. Although he was known as "Black Tom" and could be rather stern and sometimes caustic, he truly taught us how to think clearly and logically.

Aunt Hilda kindly and meticulously typed our senior theses in accordance with the mandated formatting style. Dick's thesis was entitled "Control of Consumer Credit" and mine was entitled "The Nature and Extent of Consumer Credit." The titles certainly reflected our interest in the credit business and future career choices.

Although college was very challenging, Dick and I did quite well. We received practically identical marks during our three years at Loyola. (See Appendix, pp. 110–111.) We each received honors in twenty-four semester courses during the three years. There was never a sense of competition, rather we studied together and helped each other whenever necessary. Being together provided a sense of security; it was always good for me to know Dick was there and vice versa.

On Sunday afternoon, July 24, 1949, Dick and I graduated from Loyola. The ceremony was held on the college athletic field and the speaker was Francis J. Myers, U.S. senator from Pennsylvania. (See Appendix, pp. 112–113.) Not surprisingly, I cannot recall any details of his speech! We both graduated cum laude with Bachelor of Science degrees in business administration and the equivalent of a minor in philosophy, the hallmark of a Jesuit education. We were two of only three honor graduates in the class of 110 students.

We were the first college graduates in the Horrigan family and the second and third graduates, after our cousin Joan Cunningham, in the Rauen family. Many members of the family were there for the celebration. The weekend festivities included time at Brown's Cove on Friday and Saturday prior to the graduation ceremony. Guests stayed at Aunt Anna's house, Brown's Cove and the Lord Baltimore

Hotel. A good time was had by all.

Dick and I appreciated the opportunity to attend Loyola College and were forever thankful to Mom and Pop for their sacrifices, support and encouragement. We were also grateful to Aunt Anna for providing us with the wonderful living environment, which greatly contributed to our success at school.

Shortly before Pop retired, he gave me his ledger in which were recorded the expenses Dick and I incurred during our three years at Loyola. This included tuition, books, room and board to Aunt Anna, and all our personal expenses. (See Appendix, pp. 114–118.)

An Aunt Anna anecdote: In the spring of 1971, Aunt Evelyn called to tell us that Aunt Anna had a lapsed car insurance policy. Given Aunt Anna's age, Aunt Evelyn believed she should no longer be driving. She said that Dick and I were probably the only people Aunt Anna would listen to relative to giving up her license and automobile. The following day we drove to Baltimore in my car with the intention of Dick driving her car back to Reading for resale. Initially Aunt Anna indicated that she *did* have insurance, but we insisted on seeing the policy, which she could not produce. She reluctantly agreed to give Dick her car keys. Aunt Anna asked Dick, "What are you going to do with the car?" Dick said he would sell it. She then asked Dick, "What are you going to do with the money?" to which he replied, "I will send the money back to you." Dick then asked Aunt Anna, "What will you do with the money?" She said, "I will buy another car!"

Aunt Anna remained a very important person in our lives. Dick and I had lunch with her every year thereafter on her birthday, December 19th. In 1972, Dick and I took Aunt Anna to her retirement home—Holy Family Manor in Bethlehem, Pennsylvania—where she resided until she died on November 2, 1976.

Years later when Dick and I were adults, Pop shared

with us the financial circumstances he had experienced during the 1930s and 1940s. During the Depression years of the 1930s, his income from financing automobiles was limited but sufficient to support our family reasonably well, though always frugally. As World War II unfolded in the 1940s, Detroit switched from manufacturing automobiles to the manufacture of tanks and other armaments. As a result, the war years of the 1940s were extremely difficult for Pop, with no new cars to finance. In time, the financial reserves he had developed over the years dwindled and he owed the bank money. He sought employment with the federal government to aid in the war effort, but to no avail. Pop was prepared to lay off his only remaining employee, his secretary, Ms. Heine, but she asked that he keep her on the payroll for as little as $10 a week, which he agreed to do. In the spring of 1946, Pop told the bank he wanted to provide a college education for all his children, starting with Dick and me that fall. The bank responded positively and suggested he continue to draw on his account as necessary, even though he was then thousands of dollars in the red. Also, with the war over, Detroit was retooling to manufacture cars again and the automobile finance business would soon flourish. In time, the bank's patience and Pop's perseverance were rewarded.

Pop's family. *Front row*: Mary, John, John (Pop's father). *Second row:* Myrtle. *Third row:* Evelyn, Hanna (Pop's mother) (1905)

Mom's family. *Front row:* Ed, Tom. *Second row:* Joe, Madeline, Peg, John. *Third row:* Esther, Theresa (Mom's mother), Hilda, John (Mom's father), and Claire (1908)

Mom and Pop's wedding party (1928)

Mom and Pop (1930)

Uncle Walter, B&O Railroad
police officer (1941)

Aunt Anna (1960)

Uncle Walter (right) and George "Doughy" Winterling
at Coney Island, New York (July 4, 1928)

Dick and Jack with Uncle Walter (1929)

Jack with Aunt Peg;
Dick with Aunt Claire (1929)

Dick and Jack (1929)

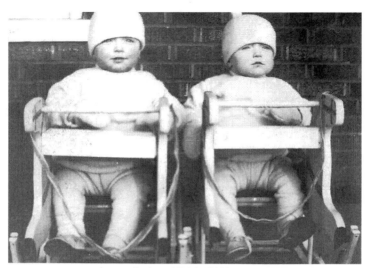

Jack and Dick (1930)

Jack and Dick (1930)

Dick, Mom and Jack (1930)

Jack, Pop and Dick (1930)

Jack and Dick (1930)

*Front row:* Dick, Mary.
*Second row:* Jack, Mom (1930)

Dick and Jack (1931)

Dick and Jack (Christmas 1931)

*Front row:* Theresa, Rosemary, Mary.
*Second row:* Dick, Joan Wertz, Bud Wertz, Jean Wertz, Jack (1933)

Dick and Jack (1933)

Dick, Pop and Jack (1933)

Dick and Jack (1933)

Mary, Pop, Dick, Jack, Theresa, Mom (1933)

Mary, Theresa, Mom, Dick, Jack (1934)

Dick, Jack, Theresa, Mary (1934)

Mary's First Communion with Dick and Jack (1937)

Jack and Dick (1938)

Dick and Maddie (1939)

*Front row:* Mary, Maddie, Peggy, Theresa.
*Second row:* Dick, Jack (Christmas 1939)

Jack, Jerry Cunningham and Dick
at Brown's Cove (1941)

Dick, Jerry and Jack (1941)

*Front row:* Theresa, Bobby Blakey, Peggy, Maddie, Lewis Blakey, Margaret Griffiths. *Second row:* Jack, Mary, Jerry, Ann Griffiths, Dick (1941)

*Front row:* Dick, Uncle John, Jack. *Second row:* Peggy, Tim Jaggers, Theresa. *Back row:* Mary, Susan Donaldson, John and Tat Walker (1941)

*Front row:* Maddie, Sue, Peggy. *Second row:* Theresa, Mary. *Back row:* Jack, Dick (1941)

Dick (front left), Jack (front center) and friends
from Exeter Junior High School playing ball (1941)

*Front row:* Peggy, Sue, Maddie. *Second row:* Theresa.
*Back row:* Dick, Mary, Jack (Christmas 1942)

St. Catharine's baseball team. *Front row:* Jack (fifth) and Dick (seventh) from left.
*Second row:* Jerry as team manager (fifth from left) (1944)

Dick and Jack, Central Catholic High School (CCHS) basketball (1945)

*First row:* Manager R. Kase, R. Horrigan, R. Didyoung, J. Reedy, G. Brizek, J. Vogel, Manager J. McFadden. *Second row:* Coach J. Schaaf, P. Gehringer, T. Powers, J. Horrigan, J. Fromuth, C. Binder, C. Tulley, Asst. Coach Father Dombay. *Third row:* J. Gallen, R. Borst, S. Luksie, R. Leitham, J. Boaman, M. Golden.

CCHS' first baseball team (1945)

## Catches Cardinal Curves

Dick Horrigan has been handling Central Catholic High's pitchers with success this season and goes behind the bat again at Pendora Friday, when the Cardinals play host to Coatesville High. His twin brother, Jack, is holding down third base since Joey Fromuth suffered a broken ankle. (Eagle Staff Photo.)

Photo in the *Reading Eagle* (May 16, 1946)

Dick broadcasting results of a CCHS football game (1946)

Jack working on the CCHS *Centralma* yearbook (1946)

CCHS Varsity basketball team. *Front row:* Jim Gallen (first from left).
*Second row:* Dick (fourth) and Jack (fifth) from left (1946)

Jack Horrigan          Danny Kranis          Charles Tulley          Jimmie Gallen          Dick Horrigan

CCHS Varsity basketball team (1946)

Jack's CCHS graduation picture (1946)

Dick's CCHS graduation picture (1946)

Thanksgiving day hike with Maddie, Dick, Sue, Jack, Peggy; picture taken on a
Pensupreme billboard at 40th and Perkiomen Avenues (1947)

Loyola College Mason-Dixon Conference championship baseball team.
*Front row:* Jack (sixth from left). *Third row:* Dick (fourth from left) (1947)

Loyola intramural championship basketball team.
*Second row:* Jack (first) and Dick (fourth) from left (1949)

Loyola Out-of-Towners Club.
*Second row center:* Jack and Dick (1949)

Jack with Mike at Brown's Cove during
Loyola commencement weekend (July 1949)

Jack's Loyola graduation picture (1949)

Dick's Loyola graduation picture (1949)

Jack and Dick upon completion of first week's Army processing at Fort Meade, Maryland; photo appeared in the *Reading Eagle* (January 11, 1951)

Jack, Jim Gallen and Dick during basic training at Fort Jackson, South Carolina (February 1951)

Jack and Dick receiving certificates of graduation from Provost Marshal
General's CID School at Camp Gordon, Georgia. Photo appeared
in *The Augusta Chronicle* (October 17, 1951)

Dolores and Dick on their wedding day (November 12, 1955)

Peg and Jack on their wedding day
(April 14, 1956)

Jack and Peg, with Dick and Peg's dad,
leaving the Berkshire Hotel after their
wedding reception (April 14, 1956)

# 18

## Transition to the Working World

DICK AND I HAD ALWAYS WANTED TO WORK for Pop's finance company after graduation from Loyola. We actually had our first taste of his business in August 1947, during our first one-month break from college. Pop taught Dick and me how to complete the new automobile sales finance contracts to bring them into compliance with changes in Pennsylvania law adopted earlier that year. We accompanied Pop as he visited his larger new and used car dealers. Dick and I later visited several of the smaller dealers on our own. This experience gave us the opportunity to learn more about Pop's business, to meet many of his dealers and to apply in a practical way some of the business knowledge we were acquiring at Loyola.

Dick and I knew that Pop had previously rejected requests for employment from several experienced men in the finance field in anticipation of our joining him after graduation. The war was over and Detroit was again making cars. The public was war-weary and families were determined to move on with their lives. This desire resulted in the purchase of consumer goods and, after four years of limited or no new auto supply, cars were in high demand. The opportunity to expand Pop's business was real, and the three of us were ready to make it happen.

Pop decided that one of us should learn the automobile finance business from him, while the other should learn the direct lending business from an established national consumer finance company. After all, if the public had pent-up demand for durable goods such as cars, logic followed (thank you Father Higgins) that there would also be a high demand for cash loans. It was our choice as to who would go where although I don't recall how we made the actual decision. In retrospect, based upon the subsequent success Dick experienced in the automobile finance business and I in the direct lending business, the right decision was made for Dick to work for Pop and for me to seek employment with a national consumer finance company. Dick always enjoyed financing automobiles, even when he had his own dealerships. Among my business responsibilities, I most enjoyed building a chain of direct consumer loan offices.

Several consumer finance companies had been identified, and Household Finance Company (HFC), with an established and highly regarded training program, became the preferred choice. At that time, consumer finance companies were the primary providers of direct cash loans to individuals, while automobile finance companies were the principal source of credit for the purchase of automobiles.

The first day after graduation weekend, en route to Philadelphia, Dick and I stopped at a phone booth to call a local HFC office, asking how best to proceed in my search for a position with the company. The receptionist suggested I visit the HFC eastern U.S. headquarters on Walnut Street in Philadelphia. Upon entering the building, I was directed to the office of the eastern regional senior vice president of personnel, Mr. Duncan. He asked why I had come to the regional headquarters since applicants are typically interviewed at the branch-office level. I explained that I was a recent Loyola graduate, that my dad was in the automobile finance business, and that I was seeking a position with HFC, the leading company in the consumer finance industry. He insisted that what I really wanted was to learn the direct lending business from HFC and then take that experience to Pop's company. I insisted otherwise and said that while my brother planned to work with my dad, I wanted to work for a large national company such as HFC. Somewhat to my surprise, Mr. Duncan arranged for me to take the HFC aptitude test the following day.

Having done well on the test, I was advised of a potential opening at one of the HFC branch offices in Philadelphia. Two interviews followed—one with Ed Bradley, a branch manager, and the second, with Mr. Jacoby, general supervisor for all eastern U.S. HFC offices. Mr. Jacoby questioned my true intentions for seeking employment with HFC, and I reiterated what I had told Mr. Duncan, that I wanted to work for HFC as the leader in the industry. Ultimately I was hired as an adjustor/collector at the 52nd and Chestnut Street branch office in West Philadelphia, working for Mr. Bradley. My monthly salary was $155, which was $10 more a month than the usual starting salary. Thus began my career with HFC.

I located a room for $8 a week in Upper Darby, Philadelphia, a short bus ride on Long Lane from my room to the HFC office. I participated in a one-week training program at the HFC regional headquarters prior to joining Mr. Bradley in early August 1949. Since I did not have a car I was identified as a "foot-man" adjustor and given a Philadelphia Transportation Company (PTC) guidebook that showed all the bus, trolley, subway and train transportation routes in the area. PTC was a very efficient public transportation system and at the time considered one of the best in the country. I learned quickly how to adjust delinquent accounts, look up and approve credit applications and in general how the consumer finance business functioned.

During this time, Dick and I opened a joint checking account and purchased a 1949 hardtop yellow and black Ford Crestliner, a very sporting young man's car. Since I was living in Philadelphia with no need for a car and certainly no means to pay for one, Dick kept the car at home with him in Reading. The joint use of "our car" in Dick's name and paid for from his earnings is a further reflection of the uniqueness of our relationship.

Since my workweek at HFC was five and a half days, I generally boarded a train late Saturday mornings and met Dick at the Franklin Street Station in Reading several hours later. Dick and I spent weekends at home, usually double-dating on Saturday evenings. Following Sunday evening dinner, Dick would drive me to Norristown where I boarded a Red Line train bound for the 69th Street Terminal in West Philadelphia. From the terminal I walked about a mile and a half to my room in Upper Darby.

A small world coincidence: Mr. Jacoby, the HFC general supervisor who recommended my being hired by HFC, was the brother of Mrs. Gehrke, the widow in Reiffton for whom Dick and I had been weekly gardeners. You never know when your past will meet you in the present, perhaps even more so today in the world of social media.

While working in Philadelphia, Dick, Mary, her fiancé Bob O'Connell and I would spend occasional summer weekends visiting a former college classmate of Mary's at her family's vacation cottage on Long Beach Island, New Jersey. We enjoyed clamming, swimming, digging for soft-shell crabs, evening cookouts on the beach and driving in Bob's 1947 Dodge—always memorable weekends.

It was during this time while living apart that our sixth-sense for each other's well-being became apparent. One morning while working in Philadelphia, I sensed that something was wrong with Dick and called Mom to ask about him. She told me he was sick in bed. Although I cannot explain how I knew it, it was probably because Dick and I had always been together during the previous twenty-one years and as twin brothers had a mutual sensitivity for each other.

During the summer of 1950, an HFC associate and I frequently attended Phillies baseball games at Shibe Park. The games were generally sold out since the "Whiz Kids," as they were known, were on their way to winning the National League championship en route to their first World Series since 1915.

Coincidentally, Pop attended the first 1915 World Series game played on October 8, 1915, in Philadelphia between the Phillies and the Boston Red Sox with Monsignor Murray, his pastor from St. Elizabeth Church. Pop served most of Msgr. Murray's 6:00 A.M. Masses and apparently the trip to the World Series was his reward. Hall of Fame pitcher Grover Cleveland Alexander was on the mound for the Phillies that day and the legendary Babe Ruth made his only Series appearance as a pinch hitter for the Red Sox. The Phillies won the game 3 to 1, but lost the series 4 games to 1.

One evening in early January 1951, Dick and I were returning from a visit with friends in Perth Amboy, New Jersey. Dick was driving and I was half-asleep beside him in the front seat when we hit an icy spot and the car spun completely around. Fortunately we came safely to a stop with no damage, except to our nerves. Understandably, Dick asked me to complete the drive back to Reading. This was the closest to being in an automobile accident we had ever experienced.

One of our friends from Perth Amboy told us about an extremely funny stage act in New York. The act involved two very different men—one debonair and mellow-voiced with an array of popular tunes, the other rather earnest and flappy-eared with a voice that would make you cringe. Their comedy together was amazing—quite different and very entertaining. This was the team of Dean Martin and Jerry Lewis at the very beginning of their careers. Several days later I had the opportunity to see Martin and Lewis on stage at the Tower Theater in Upper Darby. They were indeed hilarious and relatively unknown, but not for long.

About ten months later I was promoted to assistant manager of the HFC office at 4400 Paul Street in Northeast Philadelphia, and while there substantially increased my knowledge of the consumer finance business. The manager, whose name I cannot recall, was rather young and more aggressive than Mr. Bradley; he was also a good teacher. He was later transferred to London to open a series of HFC offices in the United Kingdom. During this time I moved to the home of Dr. John and Marie Connolly in Mt. Airy near Germantown in Northwest Philadelphia. The Connollys were very close personal friends of Mom and Pop. Needless to say the time living with them was far more comfortable than my living in a room in Upper Darby. The good times included excellent meals, gin rummy games with Dr. Connolly, watching sports on TV and a bedroom with a private bath. What luxuries!

While I was working for HFC, Dick was living at home being schooled in the automobile finance business by Pop— considered by many to be a legend in the industry. Pop had been financing automobiles, representing various companies, since the inception of the industry in the early 1920s. Who better to teach Dick the intricacies and nuances of the very competitive and difficult business than Pop? I can attest to Dick's automobile finance and management skills and Pop's teaching expertise by the many years Pop, Dick and I worked successfully together following our two-year Army hitches.

The Korean War began on June 25, 1950, and several months later Dick and I received our draft notices—as did Jimmy Gallen—requiring a physical at the New Cumberland Army Base near Harrisburg, Pennsylvania. We passed the physicals and awaited notice of when we were to be drafted. As luck would have it, I was the last person designated for the January 1951 cohort of draftees; Dick was to be drafted the following month. Dick then appealed to the local draft board, asking to be called in January so he and I could go at the same time. His request was granted and our mutual draft date was set for January 4, 1951. No doubt this was one of the few times in the history of the U.S. draft that anyone volunteered to be drafted—an oxymoron if ever there was one.

In anticipation of our going into the service, my career with HFC ended shortly before Christmas 1950, and Dick's budding career in the auto finance business was put on hold. I remember the good times we had during the last few weeks at home that year, including the usual holiday events, a New Year's Eve party and other festivities. I also vividly recall Mom's being sick and frequently lying on the living room sofa over the New Year's holiday weekend. Upon further reflection, Dick and I realized that Mom's feeling badly was directly related to our being drafted and possibly having to serve in Korea, where so many young draftees were placed in harm's way. We were neither particularly patriotic nor anxious to go, but having been in college, where about 80 percent of our classmates had served during World War II, we appreciated their sacrifices and understood why it was now "our turn."

# 19

## We're in the Army Now

POP DROVE DICK AND ME TO THE FRANKLIN STREET RAILROAD STATION in Reading on the morning of Monday, January 4, 1951. Our Army careers began at the age of twenty-two with a bus trip from there to the New Cumberland Army Base, where we had received physicals in the fall of 1950. Jimmy Gallen was with us and he provided the usual levity he was so capable of creating—a wonderful diversion then and on many occasions later. Shortly after arriving at New Cumberland we transferred to another bus bound for Fort Meade, Maryland, to begin a week of processing prior to basic training. Arriving at Fort Meade rather late on the evening of January 4th, we were introduced to our first Army meal—cold hot dogs and sauerkraut. Ugh!

Two new programs had been introduced in the Army at that time. The first was the establishment of the Scientific and Professional Personnel (SPP) program, headquartered at Fort Myer, Virginia. The purpose of the SPP program was to identify new draftees with unique educational and/or work experiences that might qualify them for other needed positions in the Army, rather than as raw infantrymen. The second program entailed the integration of white and black soldiers. In 1951, while the civil rights initiatives introduced by Presidents Kennedy and Johnson were still more than a decade away, the military was ahead of its time in recognizing the need and benefit of integrated armed forces.

During the week at Fort Meade we began the process of becoming soldiers by receiving our Army clothing, having our hair cut military style, attending numerous lectures, receiving physicals, marching in cadence and, for some of the recruits, taking a multitude of tests and interviews for those deemed to be potential SPP candidates. Jimmy, Dick and I were designated to participate in testing for the SPP program. This meant that at the conclusion of six weeks of basic training we would, if accepted, be transferred to Fort Myer for assignments based upon military needs and our skills stemming from educational and work experience.

One evening during the week at Fort Meade, Jimmy, Dick and I were playing cards on a top bunk in the barracks with several other draftees, when a corporal we did not know walked in. Jimmy inappropriately asked what we could do for him, and he replied, "Come with me." We were told to paint an enclosed bedroom in the corner of the barracks. Dick was on a ladder rolling paint onto the ceiling when he called down to Jimmy, "Damn it Gallen, don't ever open your big mouth again!" Dick expressed the feelings we all shared.

After the week of orientation, Jimmy, Dick and I were advised we qualified for the SPP program and would return to Fort Myer for new assignments after basic training. We then boarded a train to Fort Jackson, South Carolina, for six weeks of basic training. On arrival we were greeted by Sergeant Brinkley, a stereotypical first sergeant if ever there was one. During basic we learned hand-to-hand combat, how to fire M1 rifles and use bayonets, how to crawl long distances under live fire, how to grind through obstacle courses and how to march, march, march! We also had classroom sessions on military life and responsibilities, donated blood for the first time with no questions asked and learned to eat Army food. We also learned to like and very much respect Sergeant Brinkley, a fine soldier and mentor. By the end of the six weeks Dick and I were in the best physical shape of our lives.

During bivouac at Fort Jackson, Dick, Jimmy, a black soldier named Gaffney and I were assigned to a four-man pup tent where we slept head-to-head, two on each side, with our legs outside the tent. Gaffney asked if we had any problem with his being in the tent. We assured him it was absolutely no problem. This experience clearly reflected the potential conflicts with the newly created policy of mixing black and white soldiers and demonstrated why it was the right thing to do. Gaffney became a good friend and we wondered later if he had been sent to Korea, and, if so, whether he had survived.

Another time during basic training we marched to a small field barracks for several days of work on the shooting range. Sergeant Gurley, a recently recalled World War II veteran, was in charge. Although very angry about being recalled to service due to the Korean War, he did a good job and was liked by everyone. At 5:00 A.M. every day, Sergeant Gurley would enter the barracks and loudly blow a whistle for us to get up, shower, shave, dress and be ready for breakfast in twenty minutes. Jimmy Gallen was always the last person out of bed. On the last day of the field trip Gurley got down on his knees and blew the whistle directly into Jimmy's ear, screaming, "Damn it, Gallen, get out of bed!" There was only one Jimmy!

We ate well and became reasonably acclimated to Army life, which included drinking no beer or other alcoholic beverages. During the final week of basic training, however, we were able to secure a six-pack of near-beer from a friend at the enlisted men's club. The near-beer, with an alcohol content of less than half a percent, tasted good to us at the time.

Just prior to leaving Fort Jackson, Jimmy, Dick and I received a weekend pass. We boarded a bus to Charleston, South Carolina, and stayed in a local hotel there. We appreciated the clean sheets and enjoyed the good food at several different restaurants. Probably best of all was not having to follow any orders from our first sergeants!

At the conclusion of basic training we returned by train to Fort Myer and learned that Jimmy had been assigned to an Army finance office at Fort Belvoir, Virginia, where he served the balance of his two-year Army career. He did find time in the summer of 1952 to marry his sweetheart Sarah "Snooky" Boyle, whom he had met at a party at our Reiffton home several years earlier. Dick was one of the ushers at their wedding.

# 20

# CID Training

Dᴵᴄᴋ ᴀɴᴅ ᴵ ᴡᴇʀᴇ ᴀꜱꜱɪɢɴᴇᴅ to the Fifth MP Criminal Investigation Department (CID) unit for the Washington, D.C., area, headquartered at Fort Myer. The CID was effectively the investigative arm of the Army Military Police for the Military District of Washington (MDW). Our sense was that we had been assigned to the CID based upon our experience in the finance industry, our educational backgrounds and our presumed ability to write investigative reports.

In order to qualify as CID agents Dick and I were required to be sergeants (E-5), and thus over a short period of time we received successive promotions to reach the rank of sergeant. It was also necessary to have experience as a military police officer to become a CID agent. Accordingly, in April 1951 we were assigned to the Armed Service Police Detachment (ASPD), U.S. Naval Gun Factory in Washington, D.C., for a period of thirty days. The ASPD was comprised of military police from the Army, Navy, Marines, Air Force and Coast Guard, serving as a single military police unit for the D.C. area. We performed the usual duties of uniformed military police such as night patrolling in the red light district of D.C., maintaining order wherever military personnel gathered, enforcing certain curfew regulations, and so forth. We were armed and wore an MDW patch on our uniforms, but neither of us were ever involved in any dangerous altercations that called for the use of firearms.

It was during those thirty days that Dick and I learned to drink coffee, though with cream and sugar. The first time we ever joined Mom for a cup of coffee, while home on a weekend pass, she said, "You really don't know how to drink coffee until you drink it black." Subsequently, we learned to drink coffee black, another well-learned lesson from Mom.

During our time in the ASPD, President Harry Truman recalled General Douglas MacArthur from Japan, disciplining him for insubordination during the Korean War and forcing him to resign from the Army. MacArthur was either strongly liked and admired or disliked intensively. At the time of his recall the general was a very controversial and powerful person with strong Republican political support. Several years later he became an unsuccessful presidential candidate. Reflective of his huge ego, all uniformed Army soldiers in the Washington, D.C., area were ordered to appear shoulder-to-shoulder along all the public routes the general took while in town prior to his separation from the Army. This order included General MacArthur's trip up Constitution Avenue to the Capitol prior to delivering his historic "Old Soldiers Never Die, They Just Fade Away" speech to a joint session of Congress. Dick and I were among the uniformed soldiers along Constitution Avenue able to hear the speech via speakers positioned immediately above in the trees. Neither of us was fond of General MacArthur and standing in the rain during his rather long speech cemented our personal feelings.

After concluding our ASPD duties, Dick and I were reassigned to the CID office at Fort Myer. We wore civilian clothes and were sometimes armed based upon specific assignments. A fleet of nondescript black Chevrolets was at our disposal. We quickly learned our way around D.C., as well as adjacent towns in Maryland and Virginia. We occasionally visited a military shooting range to train in the use of our side arms. It was the last time either Dick or I ever fired a weapon. Fortunately we never had to fire a pistol while in the CID other than at the shooting range and, similarly, we never had to fire an M1 rifle other than during basic training. How fortunate we were!

Another requirement to qualify as CID agents was the necessity to attend a nine-week CID school at Camp Gordon, Georgia, home base for the Army Military Police. We were assigned to the Seventy-second Criminal Investigation Course at Camp Gordon on August 6, 1951. Dick and I drove from Washington to Camp Gordon in our Ford Crestliner, stopping in Burlington, North Carolina, for a quick visit with Aunt Myrtle, Lewis and Bobby. Course requirements included report writing, investigative techniques, fingerprinting, camera utilization, pistol training, military police investigative rules and regulations, and history of the CID. There were fifty-five students, all Army MPs, in the class. Frequently, after classes and a 5:00 P.M. dinner, Dick and I played tennis on the base tennis courts. This marked the beginning of our love for the game.

On many weekends we visited various places in the area such as the University of Georgia, the city of Augusta and other sites including the nearby Augusta National Golf Club, home of the Masters Golf Tournament—certainly no admission available to curious young soldiers.

In early October 1951, the day the New York Giants defeated the Brooklyn Dodgers in a one-game playoff to win the National League pennant race, Dick and I were in the base barbershop when Colonel Howard, the commanding officer of the Base, saw us waiting for haircuts. He asked if we were the Horrigan boys. He congratulated us on being the co-honor graduates of CID Class 72 with identical grades and a final average of 96.61 percent; the first time there had ever been dual-honor graduates with identical marks. We were totally surprised and at the same time understandably proud.

We graduated from CID school on October 12, 1951. Soon thereafter Mom and Pop received a heartfelt letter dated October 18, 1951, from a mother of eleven children living in McBean, Georgia. The woman enclosed an article she had clipped from *The Augusta Chronicle* that highlighted Dick's and my achievements at Camp Gordon. She explained that she had one son in the service in Wisconsin and another son about to enter the military in two months' time. As a mother, she knew how happy it would make her to receive word about one of her sons from someone who lived nearby where he was stationed. Mom and Pop certainly appreciated the thoughtful gesture from a woman they had never met. (See Appendix, pp. 119–121.)

# 21

## CID Experiences

AFTER GRADUATING FROM CID SCHOOL, Dick and I were officially accredited as assistant criminal investigators, MOS (Military Occupational Specialty) number 1446, and returned to Washington, D.C. We lived as civilians in a rented house on 8th Street NE with four other men: Mayer Sarfan, an attorney from Newport News, Virginia, and fellow CID agent; Tom Ellis, a Loyola college classmate then working in D.C.; Bill Dewey, a friend from Girardville, Pennsylvania; and Jim Joyce, a friend of Bill's from Mauch Chunk, Pennsylvania. We had a great time, enjoying life as six single young men living in D.C.

Our duties included assisting office polygraph operators, writing investigative reports, and responding to many alleged illegal incidents by Army personnel such as robberies, extortion and assaults. Generally these activities were routine and uneventful. We worked closely with the D.C. Police Department as well as other local area police departments and government agencies. On occasion we also provided security for high-ranking Army personnel similar to the U.S. president's Secret Service detail.

Dick and I were usually teamed with a more experienced agent, though rarely on the same case. Dick's partner was frequently Agent Fitzsimmons, a prototypical Army master sergeant with civilian and military police officer experience as well as polygraph machine skills. I often partnered with First Lieutenant Bernard McCune, also an experienced military police officer. The CID unit consisted of Major William Merlo, commanding officer, Captain Nick Stanislo, personnel officer, several uniformed sergeants and corporals and about twenty CID agents.

It did not take long for Dick and me to adjust to our new military life. A telling experience involved Captain Stanislo, who criticized the grammar in a report I had written. I defended my words in the report, at which time he ordered one of the sergeants to bring a large dictionary into his office for him to determine who was correct. The result was that I was correct. He then said, "Let's put it this way, I am the captain, you are a sergeant, and my corrections to the report will stand," to which I replied, "Putting it that way, Captain, you are correct." Thereafter we had no problem with Captain Stanislo; everyone recognized how to get along with him, although it was not out of respect for the man but rather respect for his rank.

A more humorous experience was the invitation from one of the uniformed sergeants in our office for Dick, Mayer and me to join him and several of his Army buddies for a poker game. Since Dick and I had played poker before, we did rather well, while Mayer lost an entire month's pay. As a result, Mayer asked us to hold his money after payday and give him a few dollars at a time as needed. Thereafter, Mayer always had available funds, never played poker again and the sergeant never again invited us to play poker.

In the early 1950s, the "McCarthy Era" was dawning in Washington, D.C., and everyone was paranoid about the "Red Scare"—the promotion of fear of a potential rise of communism. Joseph McCarthy, U.S. senator from Wisconsin, perfected the use of scare tactics primarily to achieve his own political objectives. The Russians had annexed large parts of Eastern Europe contrary to treaty requirements and had just exploded a nuclear bomb. Tensions were quite high and fear of the Russians permeated D.C. As a result, Army personnel suspected of engaging in what was then considered illegal homosexual activity were deemed to be potential security risks subject to blackmail, and their cases were referred to the CID for investigation. Dick and I were generally teamed individually with another agent to conduct such investigations and prepare written reports. The reports were then forwarded to the suspect's commanding officer for adjudication. These procedures were not unique to the Army; rather, they applied to men and women of all branches of the military as well as federal civil service employees. Over the course of three or four years, this insult to American justice prevailed and in many cases, military enlisted personnel were dishonorably discharged from the service, officers were forced to resign their commissions and federal civil service employees lost their jobs.

This oppressive witch-hunting attitude culminated in the McCarthy hearings in 1953 and the later disgrace of Senator McCarthy, who had been exposed as nothing more than an egotistical liar and bully. The recognition of human rights, so terribly ignored at that time, eventually prevailed though not without the incurred injustice taking a terrible toll on the reputations and lives of many good and honorable Americans. It was a sad time, reflecting badly on the political mores of our country.

A memorable case Dick and I had jointly investigated involved a report from the Arlington Police Department regarding an Army lieutenant colonel seen in an Arlington park associating with a group of young local punks. Prior to our interrogating the colonel, the Arlington Police Department had provided us with his bank records, revealing a number of checks drawn to one of the punks. After further investigation and a personal interview, the colonel, a senior officer in the Army Medical Corps, acknowledged he was gay and was being blackmailed. He was a perfect gentleman, very cooperative and composed; he appeared relieved to have shared this information with us. We had spent the better part of the day with the colonel and at the conclusion of the interrogation asked if he would prefer going to Walter Reed Hospital for observation rather than returning to his Arlington apartment. He asked if we thought he might commit suicide; we replied affirmatively based upon an experience in our office several weeks earlier when a major did commit suicide following a similar interrogation. He then said, "I know who I am, don't worry. I am fine." He later resigned his commission and, I hope, enjoyed a long and productive civilian life.

One of our most interesting and certainly most mysterious investigations occurred in June 1952. As duty agents for the evening, Dick and I were ordered to the Pentagon by Major Merlo to investigate the suicide of General Francis Brink, who had allegedly killed himself earlier that day in his Pentagon office. We were told that the general had been the commanding officer of a small unit of American soldiers in French Indochina, subsequently known as Vietnam. He had recently been called back to the Pentagon. Our instructions were to identify the body and then investigate the general's background in an attempt to determine a motive for the alleged suicide. At the Pentagon we were directed to the morgue, where we saw the general's body with a bullet wound in his chest. Not knowing him personally, we identified the general by examining his dog tags. We were not shown the office where the death occurred nor did we see the weapon used in the suicide. Later investigation revealed General Brink to be a career Army officer with an impeccable record and no indication of any illegal activity or any activity contrary to normal Army rules and regulations. We never found out why the general had been recalled to Washington, nor what may have been discussed (or with whom) prior to his death. Our investigative report indicated that the general had an excellent reputation in the military, was in good health with no sign of depression and enjoyed an excellent personal reputation with no known motive for the suicide. Several months later we asked Major Merlo if he had heard anything further regarding the report or had any request for more information. He replied, "We have heard nothing nor will we. The case is closed."

Dick and I had always wondered if there might have been a disagreement between General Brink and his superiors in the Pentagon as to the present or any future deployment of U.S. troops in French Indochina. Clearly there had been no indication of poor health, nor any evidence of illegal activity that may have caused him to commit suicide. Also, there was no suicide note uncovered. Was there some other reason for his death? It was a mystery that we had no opportunity to pursue at the time. Searching recently on the Internet, I found a "military corruption" website that strongly contends that General Brink was murdered because his opinions were unpopular and he knew too much. We'll never know!

Our first security assignment was for Lester Pearson, Canadian ambassador to the United States, who attended a reception and dinner at the British embassy for about five hours while we sat in the car. There must have been a particular reason why we were assigned to this detail; we concluded that most likely it was because Pearson was a very prominent official. Pearson later became Canadian minister of external affairs, Canadian ambassador to the United Nations and ultimately prime minister of Canada.

Dick and I were involved with two security details for General Dwight "Ike" Eisenhower. The first was in November 1951 when President Truman called Ike back to Washington from Supreme Headquarters Allied Powers Europe (SHAPE).

At that time there had been speculation about Eisenhower running for president in 1952, although no one knew for which party. Clearly, however, the Republican Party appeared to have the edge. General and Mrs. Eisenhower had a suite of rooms on the twelfth floor of the Stattler Hotel in D.C., together with additional rooms for his military aides and advisors. Whenever the general left the hotel, one or more armed CID agents were assigned to be with him. Also, an agent remained at the door of the suite whenever the general was inside or if Mrs. Eisenhower was there alone. I recall standing outside the suite several evenings screening whoever came to the door to see the general.

Among the more prominent of Eisenhower's guests was Judge Fred Vincent, chief justice of the Supreme Court. Addressing me rather brusquely, Judge Vincent said he was a bridge partner of the general. He walked by me, opening the door to the general's reception area himself. I never entered the suite, always remaining outside in the hall by the door.

Another recognizable dignitary was Senator James Duff from Pennsylvania. He came with several other senators on behalf of the Republican Party to urge General Eisenhower to become the Republican Presidential candidate in 1952.

The third dignitary was Bernard Baruch, a successful Wall Street businessman, known as an advisor to presidents. He was a tall, dignified gentleman whom I recognized immediately. He introduced himself to me and politely asked if he could see the general. No doubt he was an advisor to General Eisenhower in addition to being a bridge-playing friend. Ike met him at the door and I could hear them talking in the reception room of the suite since Ike spoke rather loudly. General Eisenhower told Mr. Baruch that prior to the 1948 presidential election Truman had asked him to run for president on the Democratic ticket, in which case he would not seek reelection. Ike declined and in 1948 Truman chose to run and was reelected in a very tight race against the Republican presidential candidate, Thomas Dewey, from New

York. That was the election that surprised everyone since late on election-day evening, Dewey was declared the winner only to have the later talley of votes turn the tide in favor of President Truman. The fact that Truman had offered to step aside in favor of Eisenhower in 1948 was not publicly known at the time I heard them speaking—quite a surprise. However, the fact was corroborated in one of Mr. Baruch's later books and in other historical records of the era.

Only one newsperson, representing all the news media of the day, was allowed entry to the twelfth floor of the Stattler Hotel. This is most certainly different from today's bull rush of reporters seeking information from almost anyone, the vast majority of whom are substantially less prominent than was General Eisenhower.

The second time the general returned to Washington was in the early spring of 1952. At that time he was to be separated from the Army and become an active Republican candidate for president. It was a very interesting time to say the least. Again Dick and I, as well as many other CID agents, were assigned to multiple security details during the general's stay at the Stattler Hotel.

I had the opportunity on one occasion to accompany General Eisenhower on the elevator to the lobby of the hotel. During the descent he asked one of his aides, Colonel Paul Carroll, "What is the agenda for the day?" The colonel indicated they were going to breakfast with W. Averell Harriman —a businessman, diplomat and an advisor to presidents— and then to Walter Reed Hospital to attend to a problem the general was having with his eyes. That was the extent of any close contact I had with the general, other than seeing and hearing him from outside the entry door to his hotel suite.

I recall having a very interesting conversation while at the hotel with Kevin McCann, then president of Defiance College in Ohio, who was a personal friend of the general and the ghostwriter for Ike's book *Crusade in Europe*. When giving assignments during the first Eisenhower visit the previous November, Major Merlo had suggested we read the book to better understand all that the general had accomplished. I asked Mr. McCann his thoughts about Eisenhower's entering the political arena. He replied, "I don't like it and he is too nice a person to be entering the political world." Interestingly, history has shown that Ike was indeed a good politician both in the military and in the White House.

Dick was one of the agents assigned to accompany General Eisenhower for his official separation from the Army. After the separation ceremony, Secret Service agents assumed security responsibilities for the general, and all CID agents, including Dick and me, returned to normal duties.

In the spring of 1952, Dick and I also provided security for General Matthew Ridgway, the senior officer of the Army's Far East command in Japan, who was being transferred to Paris to succeed General Eisenhower at SHAPE. General Ridgway was accompanied by his wife, Penny, their three-year-old son and their nanny. Unknown to the public the entire family had received life-threatening warnings; hence CID agents were assigned to each family member the entire time the general was in D.C. prior to his moving on to SHAPE headquarters in Paris.

One day Mayer Sarfan and I were assigned to provide security for Mrs. Ridgway. We met her at their Fort Myer residence as her chauffeur-driven military vehicle picked her up for a day of shopping; we followed in a nondescript black Chevrolet. Mrs. Ridgway stopped first at a high-fashion department store, Woodward and Lothrop, in downtown D.C. and proceeded to the women's dress department. We followed her to the fourth floor, looking completely out of place when she entered a private dressing room out of our sight. Since Mrs. Ridgway was in a private dressing room, Mayer and I decided to go to the first floor luncheonette for a bite to eat. We asked one of the dress department clerks to call us if

Mrs. Ridgway left the floor before we returned. We were clearly derelict in our duties by leaving the floor while she was there. As our lunch was being served the young woman from the dress department called to advise us that Mrs. Ridgway had left the fourth floor. Our first thought was that we would immediately be transferred to Korea were we unable to locate her. Fortunately we did find her moments later on the first floor where she was browsing through the umbrella department. Mrs. Ridgway then left the store, met her chauffeur and continued her shopping spree at numerous upscale women's stores along Connecticut Avenue. We followed in our car. Needless to say we never let her out of our sight thereafter. It was a very long and stressful day!

While Mayer and I were with Mrs. Ridgway, Dick spent the day with her son and the nanny. They visited a local playground and had a nice, quiet lunch. Dick told me he had a delightful day and had a lot of fun playing with the youngster. How different our experiences were that day!

That evening Dick and I, together with several other CID agents, were assigned as security for General Ridgway and his wife as they attended a cocktail reception in his honor at Fort McNair in Washington. General Ridgway was obviously highly regarded since full colonels and one-star generals were parking cars. Secretary of State Dean Acheson was among the many guests. We were standing off to the side when a young woman approached Dick and me asking what we were doing there since we were in civilian clothes and seemed to be out of place. We told her we were part of the security detail for the Ridgway family. We then shared our experiences that day. Later, she told us she was a reporter for *Look*—a popular biweekly magazine at that time. In the next edition of *Look* was an extensive article about Mrs. Ridgway's shopping excursion on Connecticut Avenue. She had been buying all kinds of clothing prior to moving to Paris, the fashion capital of the world. How naïve we had been to discuss anything with the reporter; and how fortunate Mayer and I were that the general hadn't asked who had been the CID agents that accompanied his wife that day.

Our last experience with General Ridgway was the day Dick and I accompanied him to Union Station in D.C., where he met President Truman as they boarded a train for West Point. It was the only time we had personally seen President Truman. Seeing the president face-to-face was quite a thrill.

Our service with the CID in Washington during the Korean War was a remarkable and interesting experience that provided a lifetime of learning and growth for Dick and me.

We were separated from the Army on December 20, 1952.

# 22

# Returning Home

FOLLOWING OUR TIME IN THE SERVICE, Dick and I returned to
Reading eager to work with Pop and to expand the auto finance and consumer finance businesses. We lived at home,
3601 Perkiomen Avenue, until our respective marriages several years later.

Pop, Dick and I had formed a new corporation in late
1952 that was required to secure a license from the Pennsylvania Department of Banking in order to make larger
consumer loans up to $2,000. Many years later, following
several name changes, this corporation became Horrigan
American, Inc., the parent holding company for all our leas-
ing, real estate and financing operations.

In anticipation of future growth, the Reading finance office was relocated from 537 Court Street to larger offices at
135 South Fifth Street in January 1953.

Dick managed and expanded the auto finance company
segment of the business, J. F. Horrigan Co., primarily by
capitalizing on relationships he had established with many
new and used auto dealers in Berks and Montgomery coun-

ties. Dick also managed and expanded the third-party home improvement sales finance segment of the company. My efforts were focused on developing the direct lending consumer finance segment of the business. The maximum direct loan amount legally permitted under the Pennsylvania Small Loan Act was $300 until 1954 when the limit was increased to $600. In February 1953, we also began offering larger loans up to $2,000 under the Pennsylvania Consumer Discount Company Act. The combination of making larger loans and capitalizing on established third-party auto finance and home improvement finance customers resulted rather quickly in substantial growth in the direct lending portfolio.

In anticipation of the increase from $300 to $600 in 1954, the thirteen licensed "small loan" lenders in the area voluntarily created a "Lenders Exchange" to limit the overloading of consumers with too much debt. The Exchange became operational on April 1, 1954, and existed for about thirty years. The primary restriction was a two-loan limit per customer. All open accounts were entered into the Exchange and every new applicant for credit was initially cleared through the Exchange to determine how many loans the applicant had. The Lenders Exchange, which the Reading Credit Bureau managed as a separate operation, was not accessible by any other credit grantors. Similarly, licensed small-loan exchanges exclusive to licensed consumer finance companies were established throughout the United States. As president of the Exchange, I was asked to speak to the Berks County Bankers Association regarding the operation of the Exchange given the bankers' sensitivity to overloading their borrowers. How different the world of consumer credit is today.

Dick and I worked together tirelessly and seamlessly to integrate all segments of the business, resulting in enlarging the offices to accommodate an ever-expanding employee base. Those early years working with each other were among the best years of our business careers. Frequently we would skip lunch entirely or eat at our desks to keep up with the workload. We would then discuss the day's activities that evening with Pop at the dinner table.

It was during this time that Pop, Dick and I met Dan Dewald, a former credit life insurance executive from Chicago, who was working for American Casualty Insurance Company in Reading. Dan and several other local businessmen were in the process of forming a new Pennsylvania-based credit life insurance company, Security of America. They sought our participation as a local finance company in an effort to build relationships with many other statewide finance companies. We eagerly joined the group. Pop served on the company's board of directors for a short period of time, followed by Dick who remained on the board until Security of America was profitably sold many years later. As an active member of the Pennsylvania Financial Services Association, I had the opportunity to solicit the credit life insurance business of many Association members. The combination of this activity and the business our finance company provided resulted in Pop, Dick and me owning a fair number of shares of Security of America stock prior to the company's sale.

Dick and I quickly learned from experience about two major risks in the automobile finance business.

The first risk is wholesale financing, the funding of a dealer's new and used car inventory prior to sale. In late December 1955, when Pop was in the hospital and out of the office for several weeks, Dick and I received a phone call from Sam Liever, a prominent local attorney. He was representing Kline Motors from Hamburg, Pennsylvania, one of our car dealers that was "out of trust"—they had failed to pay J. F. Horrigan Co. for several sold vehicles. We accepted Mr. Liever's promise that Kline Motors would pay for the sold cars by the first working day in January. When payment was not received by January 4, 1956, we began the process of repossessing Kline Motors' inventory of twelve new vehicles. Shortly thereafter we received a threatening call from Mr. Liever, saying among other things, "If your Dad were in the office you wouldn't be removing the inventory from the dealership. He is a gentleman and would have called me first. And I know who the five men are that are taking the cars and I'll have them arrested." Notwithstanding the threat, all the cars were repossessed and stored safely at another site. Kline Motors filed bankruptcy the next day and challenged our legal rights to repossess the vehicles under the 1954 Pennsylvania Uniform Commercial Code (PUCC). (Pennsylvania had been the first state in the country to adopt the Uniform Commercial Code, which was later adopted by all the states.) On November 7, 1956, Bankruptcy Judge Russell Hiller affirmed our rights under the PUCC to have repossessed the cars, giving J. F. Horrigan Co. legal authority to sell the vehicles. We thus set a legal precedent as the first automobile finance company to have properly repossessed an inventory of wholesale-financed vehicles under the Uniform Commercial Code.

The second risk inherent in the automobile finance business is the funding of contracts on a recourse basis, whereby if the sold vehicle is ultimately repossessed the selling dealer is obligated to pay off the contract. Unfortunately at times it is expected that the finance company will purchase all contracts regardless of credit. For example, Dick and I had financed on a recourse basis a number of new Ford automobiles and trucks sold to a band of Gypsies. After they defaulted, we had to scour the country for months attempting to locate and repossess the vehicles, with only modest success. Another memorable experience was our financing, on a recourse basis, of a fleet of new Ford taxicabs sold to Charlie's Cabs of Reading. Immediately after repossessing the fleet of taxicabs for nonpayment, we received a phone call from Jersey Joe Walcott, former world heavyweight boxing champion, claiming to be a silent partner in

Charlie's Cabs. He threatened bodily harm if we did not return the cabs to the company. We never returned the cabs, and fortunately we never heard from Jersey Joe again.

During the 1950s, the Reading Automobile Dealers Association sponsored an annual golf outing and gin rummy game at the Reading Country Club, followed by dinner and the Association's annual meeting. Since we were the largest automobile finance company in the area, Pop, Dick and I were invited to attend. Pop participated in the afternoon gin rummy game, and we joined him after work for the dinner. The Association president opened the meeting by telling several off-color jokes, at which time Pop said, "Let's go boys!" The three of us left the club without saying anything. At the following year's dinner, the Association president began his remarks by specifically thanking us for being there and promised no more off-color jokes. This was quite a testament to Pop's character and the respect people had for him.

One night during Christmas week in 1954 Mom and Pop were at a party with friends and returned home about midnight. Dick and I had been asleep when Mom awakened me—my bed was closer to the bedroom door. She asked that I drive Pop's car into the garage since he was having difficulty doing so. As I walked through the dining room on the way to the garage, I saw Pop. He asked what I was doing, and I told him I was going to drive his car into the garage. He told me to go upstairs and awaken Dick. When I asked why, he replied, "Why should only you lose sleep? Dick should too!" As humorous as this was, it also reflected Pop's innate sense of fairness—a hallmark of his character.

Socially during this time, Dick and I often double-dated and frequently entertained friends in the basement of our home. Three of our good buddies were Jimmy Gallen, Tom Buckley and Ed Loder. Among the favorite restaurants and bars we frequented on Saturday nights were the Crystal Restaurant and the Guard House, both in Reading, and Nick's Chat-A-While in Mt. Penn. We also enjoyed parties with Ede and Frank Ellis at their Reiffton home or at Mountain Springs, a private club on Hill Road in Reading. They were friends of the family who, with no children of their own, greatly enjoyed the company of young people. Dick and I became friends with their niece, Ruth Vaught, who attended nursing school at St. Joseph Hospital. This friendship certainly increased the number of young ladies we had the opportunity to meet. Dick and I dated several of the nurses, but none seriously. But as good fortune would have it, it was during this time that Dick and I met and courted Dolores and Peg.

While living at home at this time, Dick and I played fast-pitch softball on the Reiffton Fire Company team, he the catcher and I, the third baseman. It was great fun—no pressure, but still rather competitive. We played our home games on the athletic field behind the Reiffton Grade School, which was adjacent to a cornfield. Our left fielder, Bob Hauder, would literally run into the cornfield on long fly balls. He would invariably emerge holding the ball, which he had presumably caught, high over his head. Always an out. Seeing the movie *Field of Dreams* years later rekindled perfectly that happy memory. Our coach was George Mathews, whom we believed offered to coach the team primarily for the opportunity to gather at the Fire Company after the game for beer and conversation—Dick and I enjoyed that as well.

Dick and I were members of an investment club that met every month at The Haven in the Hills, a bar on Spook Lane in Mt. Penn. We invested $100 monthly—a lot of money for us in those days—and participated in picking stocks and managing the portfolio of investments. We enjoyed modest success and cashed out of the club shortly before Dick's wedding.

Beginning in 1953, we began taking our family summer vacations at Mom and Pop's shore house in Ocean City, New Jersey, located at 3739/3741 Ocean Avenue. Mom, Mike and the younger girls were there for the entire summer. Pop usually stayed for several weeks; the rest of the time he would commute for long weekends. Dick and I generally visited on weekends. If there was no room at the house we would bunk at The Mallard, an inexpensive motel nearby. The routine of a Jersey shore vacation began at that time and has continued ever since for our families.

In 1954 Dick and I were invited by Jack Bertolet Sr. to join the Antietam Valley Lions Club. It was our first and only experience as members of a civic club. The Club's primary focus was to aid the blind and visually impaired. We participated in many fund-raising efforts, including walking the streets of Mt. Penn and Pennside selling brooms and sundry items. The Club met every other week at the Mt. Penn Tavern for dinner, followed by a business meeting with a topical speaker. We made many new friends through this experience—of particular note is the lasting friendship with the Bertolet family.

Shortly before Dick's wedding on November 12, 1955, we closed the joint checking account we had opened after graduation from Loyola. Reviewing the account, Dick discovered a $1,000 error in our favor, thus we were each instantly $500 ahead—his, to spend on his honeymoon and mine, to spend dating Peg. What a timely find!

Dick and Dolores went to Bermuda on their honeymoon and stayed at the Princess Hotel in Hamilton. When Peg and I married five months later, on April 14, 1956, we also went to Bermuda and stayed at the same hotel. Dick and Dolores recommended several great places for dinner. One was the lounge at the Princess Hotel, after which they suggested we say hello to the lead guitarist of the band, who had taken them for a half-day fishing trip. We did so and enjoyed a rum swizzle while listening to the music. Peg commented that the guitar player was looking rather strangely at her. After completion of the set, we introduced ourselves to him and he explained that he thought I was Dick with a different woman only a short time after his honeymoon. On another evening following dinner at a French restaurant, the French proprietress said rather confrontationally and certainly not politely, "I recognize zee face (pointing to me) but I do not recognize you (pointing to Peg)." We had many good laughs sharing those stories with Dick and Dolores. These cases of mistaken identity had occurred frequently in the past and continued for many years thereafter.

Our respective weddings were the beginning of wonderful new chapters in our lives. As Dick's best man and he, mine, we reflected upon how fortunate we were to be together for the past twenty-seven years. We knew our lives would change for the better and it was comforting to know we would always be close and forever connected.

# Epilogue

DICK AND I REMAINED VERY CLOSE while raising our families. We have been blessed with fifteen children, thirty-three grand-children, six great-grandchildren—and counting.

Dick and I never outgrew the temptation to pose as one another, even to pretend being the father of each other's young children.

When attending Sacred Heart Grade School or Holy Name High School sporting events against St. Catharine's Grade School or Central Catholic High School teams, I would hear "Hi, Mr. Horrigan" from someone I did not know, realizing the greeting had been intended for Dick. I know that Dick had similar experiences.

"Which Mr. Horrigan are you?" was a common refrain that Dick and I heard throughout our lives.

Dick and I operated our businesses with assistance and advice from each other until my retirement in 1996 and Dick's in 1997. After not having seen each other for several weeks, we would have lunch and discuss business issues or personal concerns as if we had spoken about them a few hours earlier. Our sense of mutual awareness was omni-present.

Following retirement, I visited Dick at least once every week during his extended illness until he passed away on January 17, 2013. He was truly my best friend and I miss him greatly.

Jack and Dick (1981)

# Appendix

**TWIN SONS FOR MT. PENN FOLK**

Twin sons were born to Mr. and Mrs. John F. Horrigan, 2404 Filbert street, Mt. Penn, at St., Joseph's Hospital.

Birth announcement in the *Reading Eagle* (October 16, 1928)

Second birthday party announcement in the *Reading Eagle* (October 17, 1930)

**TWINS FETED**

A party was given in honor of Jack and Dick Horrigan, twin sons of Mr. and Mrs. John Horrigan of Shillington, who celebrated their second birthday anniversary. The boys received a number of beautiful gifts. Games were played. The table was arranged with a color scheme of pink and blue. Each child received a toy as a favor and a luncheon was served.

Those present were: Mary M. Horrigan, Rosemary Rauen, Richard Moyer, Jane Rauen, Horace R. Stewart, 2d, Thomas Rauen, Agnes Connley and Joan Cunningham, of Philadelphia; Mrs. Jack Cunningham, Mrs. Theresa Rauen, Mrs. Horace E. Stewart, Misses Claire and Hilda Rauen, Carrie S. Byler, Mary Boland and Thomas Rauen.

Pop's supplemental gasoline ration card (1943)

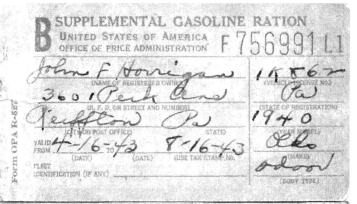

Conserve gasoline and tires. Careful upkeep and common-sense driving will increase your gasoline mileage and lengthen the life of your car.

Any person finding a lost coupon book should mail it or return it at once to the nearest War Price and Rationing Board.

☆  U. S. GOVERNMENT PRINTING OFFICE : 1942  16—28867-1

Pop's mileage ration coupons (1944)

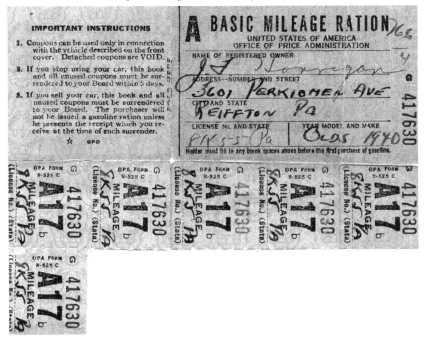

Pop's mileage ration
identification folder (1944)

UNITED STATES OF AMERICA ★ ★ OFFICE OF PRICE ADMINISTRATION
## MILEAGE RATION IDENTIFICATION FOLDER
B C T E-R

ISSUED TO *John F. Finnigan*

COMPLETE ADDRESS *3601 Perk. Ave.*

*Rifton, Pa*

VEHICLE LICENSE NO.

STATE OF REGISTRATION

YEAR MODEL AND MAKE *1940*

VALID FROM DATE BELOW *3-2-44* EARLIEST RENEWAL DATE *6-2-44* EXPIRATION DATE *Olds.*

FLEET IDENTIFICATION OR CERTIFICATE OF WAR NECESSITY NUMBER (IF ANY)

SERIAL NUMBERS OF COUPONS ISSUED
FROM: *3640944* TO: *3640956* . INCLUSIVE
COUPONS MUST BE KEPT WITH THIS FOLDER AT ALL TIMES
☆ GPO 16—37784-1

OPA FORM R-577 (REV. 12-43)

VIOLATORS OF THE GASOLINE RATIONING
REGULATIONS ARE SUBJECT TO REVOCATION
OF RATIONS AND CRIMINAL PROSECUTION
UNDER THE LAWS OF THE UNITED STATES

BULK TRANSFER AND NON-OCCUPATIONAL BOAT USE

Bulk transfer authorized? (Yes or No) _____

Non-occupational boat use authorized? (Yes or No) _____

Signed (for Board) _____ Jean Ginader

Board No. _____ County _____ Berks _____ State _____ Penna
16—37784-1

RATION HOLDER MUST
Write at once in ink or indelible pencil on face of coupons
as follows:
"B," "C," and "T."—License No. and state of registration.
FLEET CARS.—If fleet name or Certificate of War Necessity
number is used on folder, write city and State of main
office and fleet name or certificate number, instead of
license number and State of registration.
"E" and "R."—Name and address of ration holder.

ANY PERSON FINDING LOST COUPONS SHOULD
MAIL OR RETURN THEM AT ONCE TO THE
NEAREST WAR PRICE AND RATIONING BOARD

16—37784-1

Game 1 of the doubleheader between the Philadelphia A's and the New York Yankees. Pop, Dick and Jack attended the day games in Philadelphia on June 28, 1939. Lou Gehrig, having retired several weeks earlier due to his declining health, presented the Yankee lineup to the umpires before the first game and received a standing ovation from the crowd.

## Yankees 23    at    Athletics 2

| | 1 | 2 | 3 | 4 | 5 | 6 | 7 | 8 | 9 | | R | H | E |
|---|---|---|---|---|---|---|---|---|---|---|---|---|---|
| Yankees | 0 | 1 | 5 | 9 | 0 | 4 | 4 | 0 | 0 | | 23 | 27 | 1 |
| Athletics | 0 | 1 | 1 | 0 | 0 | 0 | 0 | 0 | 0 | | 2 | 7 | 3 |

| New York Yankees | AB | R | H | RBI | SO | BA | OPS | |
|---|---|---|---|---|---|---|---|---|
| Frankie Crosetti **SS** | 6 | 1 | 2 | 0 | 0 | .223 | .600 | |
| Red Rolfe **3B** | 7 | 2 | 4 | 1 | 0 | .317 | .872 | |
| Tommy Henrich **RF** | 7 | 3 | 3 | 4 | 0 | .284 | .818 | HR, 2B |
| Joe DiMaggio **CF** | 5 | 4 | 3 | 3 | 0 | .402 | 1.180 | 2-HR |
| Bill Dickey **C** | 5 | 4 | 3 | 1 | 0 | .346 | 1.016 | HR |
| Buddy Rosar **C** | 1 | 0 | 0 | 0 | 0 | .125 | .489 | |
| George Selkirk **LF** | 7 | 3 | 4 | 5 | 0 | .308 | 1.066 | HR, 2B, SB |
| Joe Gordon **2B** | 7 | 3 | 3 | 3 | 1 | .317 | .918 | HR, SB |
| Babe Dahlgren **1B** | 6 | 2 | 4 | 5 | 0 | .230 | .687 | 2-HR, SB |
| Monte Pearson **P** | 5 | 1 | 1 | 0 | 0 | .226 | .508 | |
| **Team Totals** | **56** | **23** | **27** | **22** | **1** | **.482** | **1.471** | |

| Philadelphia Athletics | AB | R | H | RBI | SO | BA | OPS | |
|---|---|---|---|---|---|---|---|---|
| Dario Lodigiani **3B** | 4 | 0 | 1 | 0 | 0 | .188 | .566 | 3B |
| Wayne Ambler **SS** | 3 | 0 | 0 | 0 | 0 | .218 | .588 | |
| Skeeter Newsome **SS** | 2 | 0 | 1 | 0 | 0 | .188 | .472 | |
| Dee Miles **RF** | 3 | 1 | 0 | 0 | 0 | .314 | .733 | |
| Bob Johnson **CF** | 4 | 0 | 1 | 0 | 0 | .315 | .989 | 2B |
| Frankie Hayes **C** | 3 | 0 | 1 | 1 | 1 | .273 | .786 | SH |
| Sam Chapman **1B** | 3 | 1 | 1 | 0 | 0 | .284 | .847 | 2B |
| Eric Tipton **LF** | 4 | 0 | 1 | 0 | 0 | .303 | .742 | GDP |
| Joe Gantenbein **2B** | 3 | 0 | 0 | 0 | 0 | .283 | .744 | |
| Lynn Nelson **P** | 1 | 0 | 1 | 1 | 0 | .313 | .677 | |
| Bill Beckmann **P** | 0 | 0 | 0 | 0 | 0 | .176 | .353 | |
| Bob Joyce **P** | 2 | 0 | 0 | 0 | 1 | .063 | .243 | |
| Bill Nagel **PH** | 1 | 0 | 0 | 0 | 0 | .267 | .788 | |
| **Team Totals** | **33** | **2** | **7** | **2** | **2** | **.212** | **.631** | |

Game 2 of the doubleheader between the Philadelphia A's and the New York Yankees. The Yankees set a record for home runs by one team in a doubleheader—eight in the first game and five in the second.

## Yankees 10    at    Athletics 0

|  | 1 | 2 | 3 | 4 | 5 | 6 | 7 | 8 | 9 | R | H | E |
|---|---|---|---|---|---|---|---|---|---|---|---|---|
| Yankees | 5 | 0 | 0 | 0 | 2 | 0 | 0 | 1 | 2 | 10 | 16 | 0 |
| Athletics | 0 | 0 | 0 | 0 | 0 | 0 | 0 | 0 | 0 | 0 | 3 | 0 |

| New York Yankees | AB | R | H | RBI | SO | BA | OPS | |
|---|---|---|---|---|---|---|---|---|
| Frankie Crosetti **SS** | 6 | 1 | 3 | 1 | 0 | .229 | .624 | HR, 2B |
| Red Rolfe **3B** | 6 | 1 | 1 | 0 | 1 | .313 | .861 | |
| Tommy Henrich **RF** | 4 | 1 | 1 | 0 | 0 | .283 | .817 | |
| Joe DiMaggio **CF** | 5 | 2 | 2 | 2 | 0 | .402 | 1.192 | HR |
| Bill Dickey **C** | 4 | 0 | 1 | 1 | 0 | .344 | 1.007 | SH |
| George Selkirk **LF** | 3 | 1 | 0 | 0 | 0 | .302 | 1.053 | |
| Joe Gordon **2B** | 5 | 3 | 3 | 4 | 0 | .323 | .954 | 2-HR, 2B |
| Babe Dahlgren **1B** | 4 | 1 | 3 | 2 | 0 | .240 | .725 | HR, 2B |
| Lefty Gomez **P** | 5 | 0 | 2 | 0 | 0 | .290 | .656 | |
| **Team Totals** | **42** | **10** | **16** | **10** | **1** | **.381** | **1.356** | |

| Philadelphia Athletics | AB | R | H | RBI | SO | BA | OPS | |
|---|---|---|---|---|---|---|---|---|
| Dario Lodigiani **3B** | 3 | 0 | 0 | 0 | 0 | .182 | .557 | |
| Wayne Ambler **SS** | 4 | 0 | 0 | 0 | 1 | .212 | .571 | |
| Dee Miles **RF** | 4 | 0 | 0 | 0 | 1 | .308 | .719 | |
| Bob Johnson **CF** | 4 | 0 | 1 | 0 | 0 | .314 | .981 | |
| Earle Brucker **C** | 3 | 0 | 0 | 0 | 0 | .261 | .800 | |
| Sam Chapman **1B** | 3 | 0 | 0 | 0 | 0 | .280 | .836 | |
| Eric Tipton **LF** | 3 | 0 | 0 | 0 | 0 | .278 | .683 | |
| Joe Gantenbein **2B** | 3 | 0 | 1 | 0 | 0 | .284 | .743 | |
| George Caster **P** | 1 | 0 | 0 | 0 | 0 | .242 | .485 | |
| Chubby Dean **P** | 2 | 0 | 1 | 0 | 0 | .296 | .692 | |
| **Team Totals** | **30** | **0** | **3** | **0** | **2** | **.100** | **.229** | |

Jack's CCHS
second semester senior year
report card (1946)

## CENTRAL CATHOLIC HIGH SCHOOL, READING, PA.

STUDENT'S REPORT, SCHOOL YEAR ENDING JUNE, 1946        (PARENT'S COPY)

REPORT OF **John F. Horrigan**        SECTION **Senior**

| PARISH **St. Catharine** | | 1st Quarter | 2nd Quarter | 3rd Quarter | Final Quarter |
|---|---|---|---|---|---|
| RELIGION  I  II  III  (IV) | | 88 | 90 | 90 | 90 |
| ENGLISH | ENGLISH  I  II  III  (IV) | 92 | 90 | 90 | 87 |
| | NEWS WRITING | | | | |
| | SPEECH | | | | |
| SOCIAL STUDIES | WORLD HISTORY | | | | |
| | MODERN EUROPEAN HISTORY | | | | |
| | AMERICAN HISTORY | | | | |
| | NATIONAL PROBLEMS | | | | |
| | ECONOMIC GEOGRAPHY — CIVICS | | | | |
| FOREIGN LANGUAGES | LATIN  I  II  III  (IV) | 91 | 91 | 92 | 92 |
| | FRENCH  I  II  III  IV | | | | |
| | GERMAN  I  II  III  IV | | | | |
| | SPANISH  I  (II)  III  IV | 92 | 94 | 92 | 90 |
| MATHEMATICS | ALGEBRA  I  II | | | | |
| | GEOMETRY — PLANE — (SOLID) | | | 90 | 94 |
| | TRIGONOMETRY | 93 | 92 | | |
| | GENERAL MATH. — BUSINESS MATH. | | | | |
| | SHOP MATH. — APPLIED MATH. | | | | |
| SCIENCES | GENERAL SCIENCE | | | | |
| | BIOLOGY | | | | |
| | CHEMISTRY | | | | |
| | PHYSICS | 88 | 90 | 90 | 85 |
| | PRE-FLIGHT — ELECTRICITY | | | | |
| BUSINESS EDUCATION | STENOGRAPHY  I  II | | | | |
| | TYPEWRITING  I  II | | | | |
| | BOOKKEEPING  I  II | | | | |
| | SECRETARIAL STUDIES | | | | |
| | OFFICE PRACTICE | | | | |
| ART | FRESHMAN | | | | |
| | VOCATIONAL  I  II  III | | | | |
| | MECHANICAL DRAWING  I  II | | | | |
| HOMEMAKING | FOODS  I  II | | | | |
| | CLOTHING  I  II | | | | |
| MUSIC  I  II  III  IV | | | | | |
| HEALTH  I  II  III  (V) | | 98 | 98 | 92 | 93 |
| PHYSICAL EDUCATION | | | | | |

104

Dick's CCHS
second semester senior year
report card (1946)

## CENTRAL CATHOLIC HIGH SCHOOL, READING, PA.

STUDENT'S REPORT, SCHOOL YEAR ENDING JUNE, **1946**     (PARENT'S COPY)

REPORT OF     SECTION

Richard W. Horrigan     Senior

| PARISH / Subject | | 1st Quarter | 2nd Quarter | 3rd Quarter | Final Quarter |
|---|---|---|---|---|---|
| St. Catharine | | | | | |
| RELIGION I II III (IV) | | 86 | 90 | 90 | 93 |
| ENGLISH | ENGLISH I II III (IV) | 90 | 90 | 90 | 90 |
| | NEWS WRITING | | | | |
| | SPEECH | | | | |
| SOCIAL STUDIES | WORLD HISTORY | | | | |
| | MODERN EUROPEAN HISTORY | | | | |
| | AMERICAN HISTORY | | | | |
| | NATIONAL PROBLEMS | | | | |
| | ECONOMIC GEOGRAPHY — CIVICS | | | | |
| FOREIGN LANGUAGES | LATIN I II III (IV) | 90 | 91 | 92 | 92 |
| | FRENCH I II III IV | | | | |
| | GERMAN I II III IV | | | | |
| | SPANISH I (II) III IV | 92 | 94 | 93 | 93 |
| MATHEMATICS | ALGEBRA I II | | | | |
| | GEOMETRY — PLANE — (SOLID) | | | 92 | 92 |
| | TRIGONOMETRY | 93 | 92 | | |
| | GENERAL MATH. — BUSINESS MATH. | | | | |
| | SHOP MATH. — APPLIED MATH. | | | | |
| SCIENCES | GENERAL SCIENCE | | | | |
| | BIOLOGY | | | | |
| | CHEMISTRY | | | | |
| | PHYSICS | 90 | 90 | 92 | 94 |
| | PRE-FLIGHT — ELECTRICITY | | | | |
| BUSINESS EDUCATION | STENOGRAPHY I II | | | | |
| | TYPEWRITING I II | | | | |
| | BOOKKEEPING I II | | | | |
| | SECRETARIAL STUDIES | | | | |
| | OFFICE PRACTICE | | | | |
| ART | FRESHMAN | | | | |
| | VOCATIONAL I II III | | | | |
| | MECHANICAL DRAWING I II | | | | |
| HOMEMAKING | FOODS I II | | | | |
| | CLOTHING I II | | | | |
| MUSIC I II III IV | | | | | |
| HEALTH I II III (IV) | | 95 | 98 | 95 | 97 |
| PHYSICAL EDUCATION | | | | | |

## Jack's CCHS second semester
## senior year report card (back)

| | 1st Quarter | 2nd Quarter | 3rd Quarter | Final Quarter | TOTAL |
|---|---|---|---|---|---|
| CONDUCT | 88 | 92 | 92 | 93 | |
| DAYS ABSENT | 2 | | 1 | 2 | |
| TIMES LATE | | | 2 | 1 | |

### EXPLANATION OF MARKS

90 to 100 . . . . . . . . . . . . . . . . . . . . . . . . . . . . . . Excellent
85 to  89 . . . . . . . . . . . . . . . . . . . . . . . . . . . . Very Good
80 to  84 . . . . . . . . . . . . . . . . . . . . . . . . . . . . Good
75 to  79 . . . . . . . . . . . . . . . . . . . . . . . . . . . . Fair
70 to  74 . . . . . . . . . . . . . . . . . . . . . . . . . . . . Passing
Below 70 (F) . . . . . . . . . . . . . . . . . . . . . . . . . Failure

Certifying Mark 80: indicates lowest mark
for which college certification is possible.

| | |
|---|---|
| 1ST QUARTER | Parent's Signature . . . . . . . . . . . . . . . . . . . . (Pastor) . . . . . . . . . . . . . . . . . . . . |
| 2ND QUARTER | Parent's Signature . . . . . . . . . . . . . . . . . . . . (Pastor) . . . . . . . . . . . . . . . . . . . . |
| 3RD QUARTER | Parent's Signature . . . . . . . . . . . . . . . . . . . . (Pastor) . . . . . . . . . . . . . . . . . . . . |
| FINAL QUARTER | Parent's Signature . . . . . . . . . . . . . . . . . . . . (Pastor) . . . . . . . . . . . . . . . . . . . . |

Parents are requested to see that three hours of home study and home work be given to class preparation during afternoons or evenings which precede school days.

Study periods in school do not eliminate home work or home study, nor do they excuse a student from bringing books home regularly.

Failure is most commonly caused by neglect of home assignments.

A report is given students after every period of nine weeks.

The marks appearing on the report in any subject are the averages of three marks given respectively for classwork, homework, and test in that subject.

Absentees must bring a written note from parents or guardians.

# Dick's CCHS second semester
## senior year report card (back)

|  | 1st Quarter | 2nd Quarter | 3rd Quarter | Final Quarter | TOTAL |
|---|---|---|---|---|---|
| CONDUCT | 88 | 92 | 92 | 93 |  |
| DAYS ABSENT |  |  | 1 | 1½ |  |
| TIMES LATE |  |  | 2 |  |  |

### EXPLANATION OF MARKS

90 to 100. . . . . . . . . . . . . . . . . . . . . . . . . . . . . Excellent
85 to 89 . . . . . . . . . . . . . . . . . . . . . . . . . . . . Very Good
80 to 84 . . . . . . . . . . . . . . . . . . . . . . . . . . . . Good
75 to 79. . . . . . . . . . . . . . . . . . . . . . . . . . . . Fair
70 to 74. . . . . . . . . . . . . . . . . . . . . . . . . . . . Passing
Below 70 (F) . . . . . . . . . . . . . . . . . . . . . . . Failure

Certifying Mark 80: indicates lowest mark
for which college certification is possible.

| 1ST QUARTER | Parent's Signature | _[signature]_ |
|---|---|---|
|  | (Pastor) | _[signature]_ |
| 2ND QUARTER | Parent's Signature | _[signature]_ |
|  | (Pastor) | _[signature]_ |
| 3RD QUARTER | Parent's Signature | _[signature]_ |
|  | (Pastor) | _[signature]_ |
| FINAL QUARTER | Parent's Signature | _[signature]_ |
|  | (Pastor) | _[signature]_ |

Parents are requested to see that three hours of home study and home work be given to class preparation during afternoons or evenings which precede school days.

Study periods in school do not eliminate home work or home study, nor do they excuse a student from bringing books home regularly.

Failure is most commonly caused by neglect of home assignments.

A report is given students after every period of nine weeks.

The marks appearing on the report in any subject are the averages of three marks given respectively for classwork, homework, and test in that subject.

Absentees must bring a written note from parents or guardians.

MONSIGNOR BORNEMANN MEMORIAL

# Central Catholic High School

# *Commencement Exercises*

JUNE 9, 1946

## Saint Paul's R.C. Church

READING, PENNA.

# Class Roll

Adams, Elizabeth A.
Adams, Theresa A.
Allen, William H.
Binder, Charles H.
Corn, William J.
Eorst, William J.
Boylan, Charles P.
Breneiser, William C.
Bruno, Dominic R.
Buckley, Thomas P.
Buniski, Anna F.
Burns, Regina M.
Chelius, Teresa A.
Cieniewicz, Stanley J.
Clausman, Robert E.
Coleman, Leonard S.
Cronan, Richard T.
Daly, Thomas F.
Davy, Marguerite H.
Dmochowski, Raymond W.
Dolan, Thomas M., Jr.
Eiler Marian L.
Eisenhower, Joan D.
Erlacher, Marie E.
Fabiani, Marie J.
Fairchild, Theresa M.
Feicht, Joseph K.
Fick, Joseph L.
Fleischmann, Geraldine M.
Franz, Helen M.
Fromuth, Joseph E.
Gallagher, Catherine E.
Gallen, James J.
Gerbino, Geraldine D.
Glowacki, Eugene A.
Golden, Charles R.
Greytok, James J.
Grossman, Esther M.

Hofmann, Elizabeth A.
Horrigan, John F.
Horrigan, Richard W.
Horting, Lytle G.
Hoyer, Dolores E.
Impink, Gerald L.
Jablonski, Mildred R.
Joyce, Patricia A.
Juranis, Clifford J.
Kane, Gerald J.
Kase, Jane L.
Kelly, John G.
Kelly, Vincent J.
Killinger, Mary Jane
Knott, Theresa C.
Kestival, William J.
Krania, Daniel J.
Krug, Lucille M.
Kurczewski, Alberta G.
Landau, Donald J.
Latshaw, Vivian E.
Leitham, Charles R., III
Looper, Frederick J.
Loeper, Jeanette A.
Loomis, Gloria C.
Luksie, Stephen E.
McDevitt, Donald G.
McQuaite, Dolores M.
McQuillen, John A.
Majka, Anthony F.
Majka, Frank P.
Maurer, Josephine A.
Miller, Theresa R.
Morin, Louis A.
Napoli, Sarah M.
Nawa, Charles R.
Nicklos, Ethel R.
Nolan, Annabelle C.
O'Reilly, James A.

Paci, Adina A.
Palick, Helen T.
Perna, Anna T.
Piontek, Arline D.
Pratzner, Stephen L.
Primeau, Donna J.
Rearden, Richard J.
Reedy, Joseph J.
Reinhard, Fred J.
Rocktashel, Richard J.
Rocktashel, Rita M.
Rowley, Jean L.
Sattler, Otto F.
Sauer, John D.
Schnable, Madeline T.
Semchock, Mary B.
Skoraszewski, Francis J.
Skoraszewski, Fred J.
Skrzyczkowski, Dolores M.
Smy, Patricia M.
Snyder, Patricia D.
Sockel, Jay B.
Souders, Harry E.
Staron, Stanley J.
Stephens, Gloria M.
Stover, Marie L.
Tobias, Richard J.
Trompetter, Walter P.
Vichio, Bernadette A.
Voelker, Elizabeth J.
Vogel, Mary F.
Vogel, Rosemary A.
Wanner, James C.
Welch, Cherie Y.
Wenger, Anne M.
Wolff, Lucy M.
Wummer, Brian A.
Zickler, Jane M.

# Class Motto

"Character is the Cornerstone of Success"

# Class Colors

Blue and White

# Class Flower

Red Rose

Jack's report card for second semester
third year of Loyola (1949)

# LOYOLA COLLEGE

4501 N. CHARLES ST.                    BALTIMORE-10, MD.

REPORT OF ........... John F. Horrigan

........... ~~1st~~ 2nd Semester ........... May 27 ........... 19 49

| SUBJECT | GRADE | EXAMINATION | SEMESTER AVERAGE |
|---|---|---|---|
| Accounting | | | |
| Architecture | | | |
| Auditing | | | |
| Biology | | | |
| Business Law | | | |
| Business Organization | | | |
| Chemistry | | | |
| Classical Literature | | | |
| Economics | | | |
| Ec. of Money and Banking | | | |
| English | | | |
| Ethics | 97 | Ex | 96 |
| French | | | |
| German | | | |
| Greek | | | |
| History | | | |
| Latin | | | |
| Mathematics | | | |
| Music Appreciation | | | |
| Natural Theology | 98 | Ex | 98 |
| Office Management | | | |
| Philosophy | | | |
| Physics | | | |
| Psychology | 98 | Ex | 96 |
| Religion | 93 | Ex | 92 |
| Sociology | | | |
| Spanish | | | |
| Ex. Mgt. | 89 | Ex | 90 |
| G&B | 93 | Ex | 95 |

### The passing grade is 65

A student whose *semester* average is 60 to 64 is permitted to take the Semester examination—to pass, the average of the examination and the Semester grade must be 65 or higher. One re-examination is permitted.

### SYMBOLS

I —Course failed due to absence.
X —Semester grade under 60 — Failure.
CON.—Failed examination — may take one re-examination ........... fee, $5.00. Students with a failure in *two* subjects are requested to withdraw from the College — if permitted to repeat the term, such students must maintain a passing average in all subjects in order to remain.

Matthew G. Sullivan, SJ
DEAN

4-47—20M—M. & T.

110

Dick's report card for second semester
third year of Loyola (1949)

## LOYOLA COLLEGE

4501 N. CHARLES ST.                    BALTIMORE-10, MD.

REPORT OF ......... Richard W. Horrigan .........

.........  ~~1st~~ 2nd Semester ......... May 27 ......... 19 49

| SUBJECT | GRADE | EXAMINATION | SEMESTER AVERAGE |
|---|---|---|---|
| Accounting | | | |
| Architecture | | | |
| Auditing | | | |
| Biology | | | |
| Business Law | | | |
| Business Organization | | | |
| Chemistry | | | |
| Classical Literature | | | |
| Economics | | | |
| Ec. of Money and Banking | | | |
| English | | | |
| Ethics | 93 | Ex | 95 |
| French | | | |
| German | | | |
| Greek | | | |
| History | | | |
| Latin | | | |
| Mathematics | | | |
| Music Appreciation | | | |
| Natural Theology | 98 | Ex | 98 |
| Office Management | | | |
| Philosophy | | | |
| Physics | | | |
| Psychology | 98 | Ex | 98 |
| Religion | 95 | Ex | 93 |
| Sociology | | | |
| Spanish | | | |
| G&B | 93 | Ex | 93 |
| Ex. Mgt. | 90 | Ex | 90 |

The passing grade is 65

A student whose *semester* average is 60 to 64 is permitted to take the Semester examination—to pass, the average of the examination and the Semester grade must be 65 or higher. One re-examination is permitted.

### SYMBOLS

I — Course failed due to absence.
X — Semester grade under 60 — Failure.
CON.—Failed examination — may take one re-examination ......... fee, $5.00.
Students with a failure in *two* subjects are requested to withdraw from the College — if permitted to repeat the term, such students must maintain a passing average in all subjects in order to remain.

*Matthew G. Sullivan, S.J.*

DEAN

4-47—20M—M. & T.

111

# Ninety-ninth Commencement

## of

## Loyola College

### Baltimore                    Maryland

## JUNE 5
## JANUARY AND JUNE CLASSES

## JULY 24
## JULY CLASS

## 1949

Ninety-ninth Commencement

Second Session

# Sunday July 24, 1949

## BACCALAUREATE MASS ............ 9:00 A. M.
### CHURCH OF SAINT IGNATIUS LOYOLA

### CELEBRANT
REVEREND MARTIN L. McNULTY, LOYOLA '09
PASTOR, SAINT CECILIA'S CHURCH

### DEACON
REVEREND VINCENT L. KEELAN, S.J., LOYOLA X'09
VICE-PRESIDENT OF GEORGETOWN PREPARATORY SCHOOL

### SUB-DEACON
REVEREND E. PAUL BETOWSKI, S.J.
FORMER PROFESSOR, LOYOLA COLLEGE

SERMON BY VERY REVEREND J. JOSEPH BLUETT, S.J.
PRESIDENT OF LOYOLA HIGH SCHOOL

## GRADUATION EXERCISES ............ 6:00 P. M.
### LOYOLA ALUMNI GYMNASIUM

### INVOCATION
REPRESENTATIVE OF HIS EXCELLENCY,
MOST REVEREND FRANCIS P. KEOUGH, D.D.

### VALEDICTORY
EDWARD F. SHEA, A.B.

## ADDRESS TO THE GRADUATES
HON. FRANCIS J. MYERS, A.B., LL.B., LL.D.
UNITED STATES SENATOR FROM PENNSYLVANIA

Pop's ledger for Jack and Dick's
Loyola expenses (1946–1947)

*Jack & Dick Expenses - Loyola College*
## TUESDAY, JANUARY 1 *1946 – 1947.*

| | | |
|---|---|---|
| May 9 1946. | Loyola Ent. Fee | 10.00 |
| July 6 1946 | " Registration | 20.00. |
| Sept 3. 1946 | " Tuition | 170.00 |
| " " | Books. | 73.00. |
| Sept 17 1946 | 2 3rd Ex | 20.00. |
| " 21 1946 | 1 wk Ex | 10.00. |
| " 28 1946 | 1 " " 10.00 | 20.00. |
| | Shoe Skates 10.00 | 60.00. |
| Oct ✓ 1946. | G.N.P. Sept 1946 | 15.00 |
| " " " | 1 wk Ex 10.00 5.00 | |
| | Mem. | 10.00 |
| " " " | Extra Ex | 170.00 |
| " 26. 1946. | Loyola - Tuition. | 20.00. |
| " 28 | Extra. Ex | 10.00 |
| Nov 2 | 1 " Ex | 10.00 |
| 9 | G.N.P. Oct 1946 | 60.00 |

## WEDNESDAY, JANUARY 2

| | | |
|---|---|---|
| 29 | 1 wk Ex to 11/16 | 10.00 |
| | 2 " " to 4/30 | 20.00 |
| | G.N.P. Nov 1946 | 60.00. |
| 16 | 2 wk Ex to 17/14 | 20.00 |
| 20 | 1 " " to 1/21 | 10.00 |
| Jan. 13. 1947 | " " " to 1/13 | 30.00 |
| 27 | 1 " " to 1/10 | 10.00. |
| | Books. | 30.00. |
| | G.N.P. Dec 1946 | 60.00. |
| | " " Coats | 6.00. |
| | Loyola Tuition. | 130.00 |
| Tea 2 | 1 wk Ex to 1/27 | 10.00) |
| 10 | G.N.P. Jan 1947 | 60.00 |
| 10 | 1 wk Ex to 2/8 | 10.00 |
| 22 | 2 wk Ex to 2/22 | 20.00 |
| 22 | 1 wk Ex | 10.00 |
| | | 1188.00 |

114

Pop's ledger for Jack and Dick's
Loyola expenses (1946–1947)

**SATURDAY, JANUARY 5**

| | | | |
|---|---|---|---|
| 9 | Feb. 1947 | Spic Port. | 17.80 |
| | 24. | ... | 2.00 |
| 10 | March 7 | Dave Ex | 20.00 |
| | | G.H.P. Feb 1947 | 60.00 |
| 11 | 14 | Loyola Tuition | 170.00 |
| 12 | 15 | Dick. Ex. | 10.00 |
| | 21 | " Ex chest 20°° | 10.00 |
| | | | 20.00 |
| 1 | 28 | Mercy Hospital (Dick) | 38.40 |
| 2 | | Dick Ex | 10.00 |
| 3 | Apr 2 | Entre & Cash Dave | 5.00 |
| | | " | 5.00 |
| 4 | 8 | 1 week Ex | 10.00 |
| | 17 | G.H.P. March 1947 | 60.00 |
| 5 | 19 | Dick. Ex | 10.00 |
| | 20 | G.H.P. ... (Dick) | 10.00 |

**SUNDAY, JANUARY 6**

| | | | |
|---|---|---|---|
| 9 | 29 | 1 week Ex | 10.00 |
| | May 5 | 1 " Ex | 10.00 |
| 10 | 11 | 1 " Ex | 10.00 |
| | 16 | 1 " Ex | 10.00 |
| 11 | 16 | G.H.P. Apr 1947 | 60.00 |
| | 26 | ... Ex | 10.00 |
| 12 | | Book | 1.00 |
| | 27 | Loyola Tuition | 170.00 |
| 1 | | Jack Watch | 8.00 |
| 2 | 31 | additional to Dick | 5.00 |
| 3 | Jun 7 | 1 week Ex | 10.00 |
| | 1,9 | G.H.P. May 1947 | 60.00 |
| 4 | 21 | ... Ex | 10.00 |
| | July 2 | ... Co. Port | 17.90 |
| 5 | 4 | 1 week Ex | 10.00 |
| | 11 | 1 " Ex 8.00 | 20.00 |
| | | ... 1.00 | 60.00 |
| | | G.H.P. Jun 1947 | |

Pop's ledger for Jack and Dick's
Loyola expenses (1947–1948)

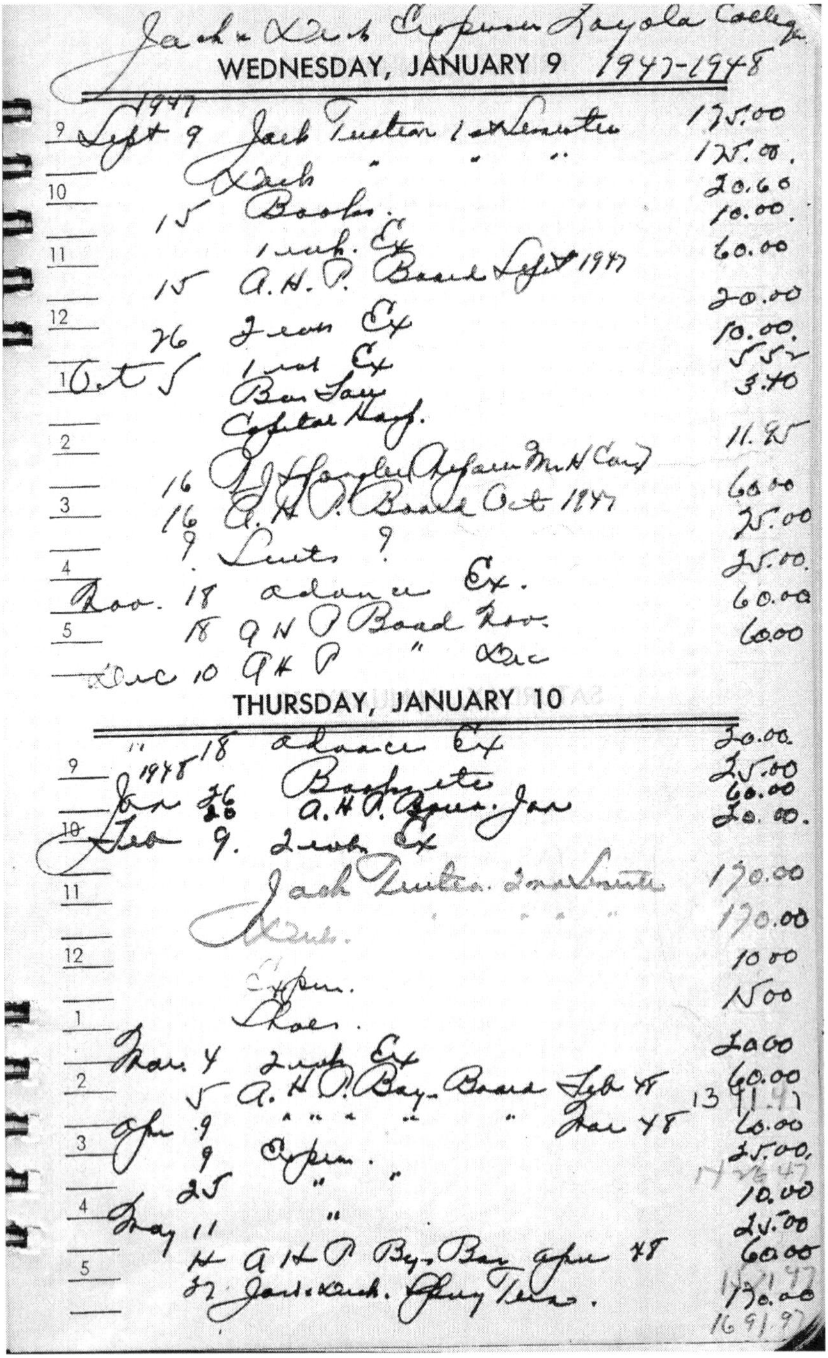

Pop's ledger for Jack and Dick's
Loyola expenses (1948–1949)

THURSDAY, JANUARY 17  1948-1949

9
10
11
12
1
2
3
4
5

FRIDAY, JANUARY 18

9
10
11
12
1
2
3
4
5

Pop's ledger for Jack and Dick's
Loyola expenses (1948–1949)

*Jack & Dick – Expenses, Loyola College*

**MONDAY, JANUARY 21** *1848–1949*

#✓. 249.00.

Jun 29   Allow.                    20.00

July 5    "                        20.00
     6    Q.H.O. May~Jun          125.00

                                  ~~224~~
                                  ~~274.00~~
                                  247⁴

*Jack & Dick.*

*Loyola College.*

1948–1949

247⁷⁰⁰

*Jack & Dick.*

**TUESDAY, JANUARY 22**

1946–1947.        2309.90
1947–1948.        1851.97.
1948–1949.        2478.00
     TOTAL        6538.87

118

Article appearing in *The Augusta Chronicle* detailing
Jack and Dick's graduation from CID School (October 17, 1951)

# Identical twins, same scores, are honor graduates at Gordon

Pvts. John F. and Richard W. Horrigan, Fifth Criminal Investigation detachment with duty station in Washington, D. C., have recently completed the Enlisted Criminal Investigators course at the Provost Marshal General's school, Camp Gordon.

As startlingly alike as any two men can be, they were the source of added consternation in the secretary's office, PMGS, upon completion of the nine weeks course— not only were they the top students for the group of 55 enrollees —they had both obtained identically the same scores, (96.61 per cent). Careful checking of points for the entire course failed to show even a fraction's difference so they completed the course as dual honor graduates.

In variance from normal procedure, duplicate letters of commendation were made instead of the usual one.

The twins were inducted into the service together on January 4, 1951, and both received basic training at Fort Jackson, S. C.

They have been jointly associated in nearly all activities since childhood. They graduated from Reading Central Catholic High school in 1946 and both completed Loyola college, Baltimore, in 1949 with B. S. degrees in business administration.

They are the sons of Mr. and Mrs. John F. Horrigan, 3601 Perkiomen avenue, Reiffton, Pa.

Letter sent to Mom and Pop from a mother
in McBean, Georgia (October 18, 1951)

M.C. Bean Ga.
Oct. 18- 1951

Dear Mr & Mrs Harrigan.
Guess you will be sup-
rized. to get a letter from a complete
stranger. But in reading my paper
yesterday - The augusta Chronicles I
read this clipping, I'm enclosing -
It is a remarkable, praise that
is offered to your, Son's. and I being
a mother with a a son in service
& one to go in Dec - Thought how happey
it would make, me to recieve, a
clipping or any, word concerning my son -
from some one, in or close around camps
where he, is or could be serving - I
think your sons are just fine, altho I
dont no either one of them personally,
But when one or two of boys in an
army camp, rates, on news paper
article, they just have to be fine -
My son in service is Wm Smith
Jr - (24783898) Btry. B. 101st A.A.B Gun
Bn - Camp Mc Coy - Wis; Black hair -
blue eyes- 5 ft - 11" wht 201 lb - also a Cook.
So just in case he ever stationed
in a Camp, close to your home, town,

120

P.S.— McBean, Ga is about 40 mile from. Camp
Gordon— Where your Sons— are.

and in turn, your paper Carrier an
article about some thing he, achieves—
I'll say from depth of my Heart
I & his Father Would greatly
appreciate your, sending it to us—
So how may we join our prayers together, that this awful conflict, may
end— very soon, & may "God's peace
& happiness, rule in place of War &
Sin" If I Come in Contact with your
Sons— I promise they will surely be
welcome, in Our home & with our
Children—as I am mother of Eleven—
— Five S. Boys— I surely no how to
love & appreciate— Children— Our son is
home on 15— day leave— now— its so
good to see him, come home— but I.
that, heart Break, to see him, have to
leave to go back— So now may God's
richest blessings, flow, on all mothers'
sons every Where— I'll say "God.
Be With you. all, & will we meet in
Heaven— some day—
　　　　　　Sincerely— a mother—
　　　Mrs Julia Quick, Sr—
　　　Mc Bean, Ga.
　　　　　　R-1

121

Made in the USA
Lexington, KY
16 November 2014